A new look at
growing old

"What Should We Do About Mom?"

Richard T. Conard, M.D.
with Jill LaForge Jones

 Human Services Institute
Bradenton, Florida

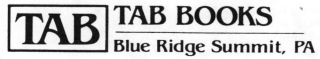 **TAB BOOKS**
Blue Ridge Summit, PA

Human Services Institute publishes books on human problems, especially those affecting families and relationships: addiction, stress, alienation, violence, parenting, gender, and health. Experts in psychology, medicine, and the social sciences have gained invaluable new knowledge about prevention and treatment, but there is a need to make this information available to the public. Human Services Institute books help bridge the information gap between experts and people with problems.

FIRST EDITION
FIRST PRINTING

Library of Congress Cataloging-in-Publication Data

Conard, Richard T.
    "What should we do about Mom?" : a new look at growing old / by Richard T. Conard.
        p.   cm.
    ISBN 0-8306-3957-8 (p)
    1. Aged—Care—United States.   2. Aged—United States—Family relations.   3. Intergenerational relations—United States.
    I. Title.
    HV1461.C664   1992
    362.6—dc20   92-15760
                                                                              CIP

Acquisitions Editor: Kimberly Tabor
Development Editor: Lee Marvin Joiner, Ph.D.
Copy Editors: Pat Holliday and Pat Hammond
Cover: Holberg Design, York, Pa.
Cover Photograph: Thompson Photography, Baltimore, Md.

Questions regarding the content of this book should be addressed to:

Human Services Institute, Inc.
P.O. Box 14610
Bradenton, FL 34280

Contents

To all the unsung heroines who, as loving children, have assumed the caregiving responsibilities for their aging parents.

Foreword

The growing number of people living to their sixties, seventies and eighties apparently has caught our youth-oriented world off balance. It has not yet accommodated to the idea of so many people living even into their nineties. Given the present demographic trend, there will be further increases in longevity——even beyond the nineties. It is projected that by the year 2025 the population count of the elderly will be around forty to fifty million.

Although many of the older sixty-, seventy- and eighty-year-olds are happy and content where they are at the present time, there are many who are afraid to move to new horizons. While they are the ones who brought us to where we are today, there is a real hesitancy about moving on in light of what is taking place in today's and tomorrow's environment. Having done it once and realized the struggle, many feel that they have paid their dues.

In today's society it is very hard for anyone to look past their own little corner. Yet we know that the only thing that is constant in this world is change. Things are going to be different and the fact must be accepted in spite of our resistance or lack of preparation for that change. Perhaps this is the greatest challenge of the 1990s: to communicate better with all age groups to ensure a better understanding of the dynamics of each group. To meet this challenge, *What Should We Do About Mom?* willingly moves past our fears and uncertainties and addresses this problem. With case studies and years of experience, the reader is given a clear picture of the difficulties brought on by the increase in our aging population, where our sociological progress has not kept pace with the technological advances.

This presentation is not a narrative account, it is a step by step "how to" with definite guidelines for meeting the problems of present day adults and elderly. In addition, there is a look at what the future holds, given further increases in the older population. Strong emphasis is placed upon looking ahead and planning, so that decisions can be made when there is no crisis or strong emotional upheaval. The need for planning, and its success, rests on good communication, which is a vital factor in addressing the interaction between present day parents and their elderly parents.

The key to a successful solution in regard to where and how frail elderly parents should be cared for, lies in what Dr. Conard calls "noninvasive intervention" and the focus is on "caring about" as much as "caring for." Making modifications in the lifestyle of the aging parent can be traumatic for both the cared for and the caregivers if the approach results in a loss of self-esteem or causes guilt feelings. Specific steps are outlined and recommendations are given to caregivers regarding their interaction with elderly parents. Sample solutions, with several options, are presented to meet diverse needs. Following the guidelines in the book can make the transition more acceptable, while still taking into account the basic human needs. The stress on planning also is directed to those who are of a younger age. If the present trend in aging continues, they will someday be eighty or ninety.

The book is timely and will be very advantageous for use in preretirement seminars. For those parents who have the duty to be caregivers to their parents, it is a clearly marked road map. In the book, there has been an attempt to include all the findings that will be helpful to all people. Not only will the suggestions help to deal with aging parents, they will help build a solid foundation of attitudes about aging. Hopefully, *What Should We Do About Mom?* it will lead to a careful evaluation of your feelings, a defining of your goals and show the importance of greater family interaction.

And so gentle reader, here is the book. Turn the ideas over in your mind, distill them through your experience and then express them through your personality. They are not meant to be salted away in some place to become history. They are meant to be impressed upon your life first, and then shared with others in your own distinctive style.

C. Kermit Phelps, Ph.D.
Past Chairman of the National Board of AARP

Acknowledgments

I wish to thank all the people in the Manatee County community who honored me by allowing me to be their family physician and from whom I gained many of the insights and experiences described in this book.

I am grateful for the professional insights of those professionals in gerontology who serve on the Advisory Board of the *National Foundation on Gerontology*, including Paul Densen, D.Sc., Barry Gurland, M.D., Leonard Hayflick, Ph.D., Betty J. Havens, M.A., Robert L. Kane, M.D., and Leon Pastalan, Ph.D. Their patience and input allowed me to accelerate my learning curve and made it a more pleasurable experience.

Many thanks to my collaborating author, Jill LaForge Jones, and to my editor, Lee Marvin Joiner, Ph.D., both of whose talents and professionalism contributed in a very significant way to the quality of this book.

I am grateful for the support my wife, Betty, and my family have given me in this endeavor, as well as that lent by my father-in-law, Dr. James McEldowny, who in himself is an inspiration.

I wish to thank Donna Painter, who encouraged me to write this book; Dr. Ed Dickerson, who first put me into medical practice in this area and who has remained a steadfast friend for over two decades; and Fred Langford, who believed in my program for elderly housing and who provided much of the financial wherewithal to allow me to pursue the medical complexes and residential retirement facilities I have developed.

This list could go on forever, for I have been blessed with so many good people in my life. If I didn't name you, it doesn't mean I didn't think of you.

Author's Note

The case studies cited in this book are from my personal experience, but I have changed the names to protect the identities of patients, residents and friends.

Although the title of this book refers to elderly women, the thoughts and ideas within these pages are applicable to any situation in which a person is a caregiver to an elderly person, whether it be a mother, father, grandparent, aunt, uncle, or even an older friend. For the sake of clarity and ease of reading, I have used the feminine gender throughout the book to represent both sexes.

Introduction

Millions of Americans, most of them women over the age of forty, many with full-time careers and children still at home, are finding themselves suddenly faced with a huge and unexpected additional challenge—caregiving responsibilities for one or more of their parents who have become too aged and too frail to manage on their own. Often, this additional responsibility creates incredible stress for the entire family. Bedrooms must be shared. Finances must be more closely watched. Vacations must be cancelled, or so it seems to most people caught up in this situation. But when a loved one needs help, who is going to say no?

Until now, there have been few guidelines for coping with caring for an aging parent. No one has written a parent care manual to guide us through this difficult period of life. Until very recently, this situation simply did not exist!

Caregiving to elderly parents, at least in the duration and intensity many are experiencing now, is a new role in the human drama. It has only been in the past few decades that people have lived long enough to need specialized care in their later years. Before the days of miracle drugs, bypass surgery, and chemotherapy, death came to most folks in their fifties, sixties or early seventies. But in the search for better health for all ages, we have both prolonged life and created a huge, unexpected problem: the elderly are living to be eighty, ninety, even over one hundred. We now have an entirely new generation of the very, very old.

Unfortunately, we have not stayed abreast of these changes and the needs they created for the care of the very, very old. As a nation, we are unprepared for the large and rapidly increasing population of Americans who are over seventy. Our health care system is inadequate and inappropriate. Our senior living facilities have not been developed to meet the continuum of care needs of the elderly. We have failed to overcome old stereotypes of aging that keep us locked into old, no longer valid beliefs.

Everyone involved is poorly prepared for what is happening. The elderly themselves often express surprise and even dismay at living to such extended ages. A woman in one of my retirement facilities recently said (at a meeting of the *Nineties Club*, which was attended by fourteen residents, almost a quarter of the total population of the home), "I never thought I'd live to be ninety. Even my sons are amazed." Then she lifted her glass of wine in a toast to good health.

Unfortunately, this woman is the exception, not the rule. She is healthy, well-adjusted and happy in an assisted living environment that allows her as much independence as she can handle, while providing support as she needs it. She and her children have worked together to find a satisfactory solution to the problem of caring for her in her very advanced years.

Not all families are so fortunate, or forward-thinking. Many have not given the future of their aging parents much thought, not because they are uncaring, but just because they have not had to face the problem of caring for the elderly before. Then, suddenly, one of their parents dies, becomes critically ill or displays inappropriate behavior, and the adult children are called upon to care for the widowed person or the one who is left in good health. Ironically, it is not usually an ill person who becomes the primary concern; it is the healthy but frail parent, now left without a life partner, who will ultimately need care, support, and a tremendous amount of loving patience from her children.

I have written this book to help those adult children of aging parents who find themselves sandwiched between the demands of childrearing, careers, and this new role of parent caregiver. You know who you are. Most of you are women in your middle years. Many of you still have teenagers living at home or are experiencing the financial drain of trying to put kids through college. A lot of you had plans for spending some quality time alone or with your spouse after the children were grown, perhaps traveling or just enjoying a peaceful, quiet household once again.

And now this. Dad is gone, and Mom can no longer live alone. Or Mom is gone, and Dad can no longer cope by himself. You turn your spouse or your siblings and ask helplessly, "What should we do about Mom?"

Perhaps this book will help you answer that question. It is my fondest hope that in sharing what I have learned over the past twenty years as a physician to elderly persons, a developer and manager of elderly housing, and a son to elderly parents, my experience will be of some assistance to you. In the following pages, I will discuss the signs to watch for if you suspect your aging parents are having problems coping with life and explain what is happening to them that might be causing the behavioral changes that sometimes make dealing with them quite trying.

I also offer solutions and, yes, there are many available. You must be prepared to take some steps that require courage and integrity so as to create the changes in their lives that will work best for both of you. You must be prepared to intervene in their lives in a noninvasive way, to communicate openly and establish a trust level that will allow them to transfer freely some of their responsibilities to you without resentment or the feeling they are no longer in control of their lives. You will learn to recognize the innocence in some of their behavior and discover ways for you and your elderly parents to work together to create solutions that are healthy for everyone involved.

Many adult children feel tremendous doubt and guilt about what they are doing to their parents when relocating them into an "old folks home." This is no longer the only option, and I outline specific suggestions for alternative living arrangements that offer many others.

Finally, I will leave you with some thoughts about your own old age so that you and your children can plan together. Perhaps by doing so, they will not experience the same traumas you are facing with your aging parents, and they won't have to ask . . . "What should we do about Mom?"

1

You Are Not Alone

The woman sitting across the desk from me had large dark circles beneath her eyes. Her face was lined and haggard. I had known her since she was a child, and I could almost guess what she was here to see me about before she opened her mouth to speak.

"It's about Mom," she began, her voice quavering.

Marge Hanson's mother was one of my patients. "Is she ill?" I asked.

The attractive, middle-aged brunette shook her head, and I could see tears brimming in her eyes. "She's not. But I think I am."

Then the words came out in torrents, describing the many sleepless nights she'd spent since her elderly mother had come to live with her family, nights filled with worry, fear, anxiety, depression, and guilt; nights spent tossing and turning, wondering if she and her husband had made the right decision to bring her mother into their home after her fall; dark lonely hours trying to overcome the resentment she felt at having her life so disrupted. The only conclusion she'd come to was: "This can't go on."

I wish I could use a tape recorder at such times, to share with people like Marge the hundreds of other similar stories I have heard from the children of my elderly patients. Marge is not alone. She is just one of millions of people today who, besides career and family obligations, find themselves suddenly having to cope with the additional responsibility of caring for their elderly parents. The media has dubbed them the "sandwich generation."

The Sandwich Generation

The Sandwich Generation is comprised primarily of women between the ages of forty and seventy, though there are some men who share much of the burden or shoulder it alone. The fact is that, despite the changes brought about by the women's movement, women are still the primary caregivers in the typical American family. It is still the woman who does most of the cooking, cleaning and child care. When an older family member needs help, it is usually the eldest daughter who gets the call. When the only child is a son, it is often the daughter-in-law to whom the older person turns for help. In a situation where no female "child" is available, a niece may become the caregiver. To compound matters, the increase in divorce may have resulted in some women having not one set of parents and in-laws to care for, but up to four! Caregivers today may find themselves feeling something like a den leader all over again, only her charges are much older than Cub Scouts!

No wonder Marge felt sick! Possibly in earlier times, caring for elderly parents didn't present the problem it does today. A hundred years ago, we were still mainly an agrarian society and most families simply integrated older family members into their rural living and working environment. Today, however, we are much more urban and suburban. Families leave the house in the morning, each person headed in a different direction. Dad goes to his job. Mom goes to hers. Teenagers are off to high school or college and possibly a part-time job. Nobody's left home to take care of Grandma. So Mom starts coming home at mid-day to check on her and make lunch. Then it's back to the office for the afternoon, but not without nagging worry in the back of her mind . . . what if she falls? What if the house catches on fire? What if? . . . What if? . . .

The women's movement changed Mom into Supermom when women embarked on careers of their own while still maintaining their traditional roles as primary caregivers to their children. Now the increasing longevity of the older generation is demanding that Supermom become Megamom by adding yet another caregiving assignment to her already full agenda.

No wonder Marge looked tired and haggard! Those women of the Sandwich Generation are most likely at the time in their lives when they expected to be nearly finished with their childrearing years and were looking forward to kicking back and enjoying life. Instead, many are faced with a whole new set of demands from an elderly parent, and few are equipped to cope with the challenges.

Teenagers who are not used to sharing their parents, much less their space, with Grandma or Grandpa sometimes turn their own anger at the situation into acting out with belligerent behavior, poor performance in school, possibly even such negative behavior as experimenting with drugs, alcohol and sex.

Marital relationships can be put severely to the test. Husbands and wives have neither the privacy they once had nor the time together to maintain intimacy. The caregiver can experience fatigue and depression because she may simply not have enough time and energy to meet the needs of everyone in a three-generation household. Financial problems resulting from trying to meet the needs of the elderly can cause tremendous emotional stress in a relationship.

If you are one of the millions caught in the Sandwich Generation, you know it can be a lonely, thankless job. If you are experiencing this overload of responsibility, it is not surprising if you are stressed out, tense, irritable and sometimes even sick. You're probably feeling ambivalent toward your parents or in-laws who have mired you in this mess. Of course you love them, but you feel trapped and frustrated. You are angry, and you probably take your anger out on those closest at hand—your spouse, children and your aging parents themselves. Unless you learn some coping skills and techniques, the cost of remaining sandwiched could be high.

This is not an easy situation, let me assure you, nor is it one that will go away any time soon. The problem is enormous and growing day by day. The elderly are rapidly becoming the largest segment of our country's population, with predictions that there will be more than thirty-five million people over the age of sixty-five by the year 2000. Only twenty years later, aging baby boomers could push that number to fifty million.

Even more astonishing to me are the statistics for those eighty-five and older. At the beginning of this century, there were just over 100,000 people in this population group. At the end, there will be an estimated five and a half million people in our country over eighty-five, and by 2020, there will be sixteen million! And for each of these elderly persons there will likely be a younger counterpart caught in the Sandwich Generation. It is a mind-boggling proposition!

Where Did They All Come From?

How is it that we find ourselves in such a dilemma? What went wrong that we are so unprepared? The answer is simple. Our scientific, medical and technological advances have moved at lightning speed and simply outstripped the ability of our social structure to keep up. Improvements in sanitation, compulsory vaccination, development of antibiotics and miracle drugs, and dramatic new surgical techniques have literally added years to our lives. Lots of years! (see table 1.1).

TABLE 1.1
Highlights of Twentieth Century
Medical Progress

Decade	Event(s)
1900s	*Improvements in sanitation and advancements in understanding of how diseases are transmitted. Also, more rigid enforcement of compulsory vaccination and the increasing availability of refrigeration for vaccine storage.*
1930s	*Advent of many antibiotics and methods to actively treat disease.*
1950s	*Breakthroughs in cardiovascular drugs.*
1970s	*Revascularization and transplanting of diseased organs.*

Since 1900, the average *life expectancy* for Americans has increased from the mid-forties to the mid-seventies, and it continues to move steadily upward (see fig. 1.1). In the early 1960s, my colleague Dr. Leonard Hayflick, a bioscientist studying human cell development, proved that human cells have a finite, limited *life span*. Until Dr. Hayflick's experimentation, it was generally believed that cells were immortal and capable of replicating themselves forever. If only science and medicine could prevent the diseases that attack human cells, we could conceivably live forever. Dr. Hayflick's studies, however, proved that human cells can tolerate only a certain number of normal coupling replications before they can no longer physiologically sustain life. Presently, many scientists and doctors agree that the life span of a human—the number of years the biological machinery can physically continue to

regenerate itself—is about ninety-five years (see fig. 1.2).
The way things are going, it is conceivable that one day,
our life expectancy may be the same as our life span (see
fig. 1.3)!

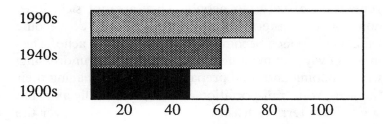

Fig. 1.1. Life expectancy trends in twentieth century.

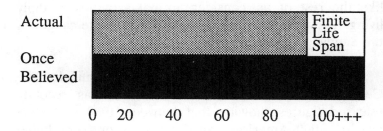

Fig. 1.2. Life span: actual and once believed.

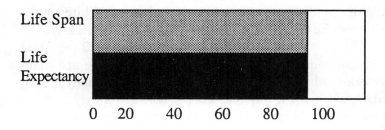

Fig. 1.3. Future possibility: life span and life expectancy.

And We Think We've Got Problems Now?

With the additional thirty-something "bonus years" we have tacked onto our life expectancy in the last century, we have created a monster of sorts—an entirely new generation of very old people. They are not sick. They don't need long-term nursing care. But they do become frail. Their bones become brittle, their joints ache. They move slowly and need help with dressing and undressing; with shopping and food preparation; with managing their finances; with transportation. Most are mentally alert but suffer from terrible frustration, even depression over the situation in which they find themselves. Formerly active, robust individuals, they find it degrading to have to depend now upon others to make it through what they, like the rest of us, consider normal activities of daily living. They are generally as unhappy as those caught in the Sandwich Generation.

Some become so unhappy they commit suicide. The Center for Disease Control in Atlanta has recently released figures showing that between 1980 and 1986 nearly 37,000 Americans aged sixty-five or older killed themselves. The overall rate suicide rate for elderly adults was 21.5 per 1000, nearly eight percent higher than the highly publicized rate of teen suicides. White males showed the highest rate of suicide among the elderly, 45.6 per 1000. Among black males the rate was 16.2 per 1000. Among white females the rate was 7.5. There are many reasons, which we will soon explore, why so many elderly are looking for a way out. People who are lonely and feel isolated and useless see no reason to go on living.

A Role For The Elderly

The time has come for us to focus on catching up with all
of our advances and reintegrate these elderly individuals
into our society. Thirty million people over the age of
sixty-five have a lot of combined experience. If each were
to live an extra twenty "bonus" years, we would have six
hundred million extra person-years that we could put to
use solving the myriad problems on our planet. The
challenge is to find a way to use this valuable resource.

One problem we face is that this generation is the only
one in our society without a definitive social role. Upon
retirement, people who have always fulfilled a specific
social role—parent, breadwinner, community leader—find
themselves for the most part suddenly without this kind of
identity. People who have, in the past, thought of themselves as productive tend to perceive themselves as nonproductive and, consequently, useless to their families, to
society and to themselves. They buy into another negative
stereotype of aging in our country: if you aren't productive, the meaningful years of your life are over. Many of
today's elderly, who equate their worth with their productivity, suffer from a severe loss of self-esteem once they
retire from their former societal roles. Much misun-
derstanding between generations occurs as a result.

When any person loses self-esteem, no matter what
age, she is likely to show certain behavioral changes, not
many of which are positive. Although it is difficult, adult
children of elderly parents need to recognize the innocence behind the behavioral changes their older loved
ones might exhibit. They are frustrated, feel unwanted,
unneeded, unable to fit in any more. They become bored,

depressed, irritable, sometimes downright cantankerous!

It is one thing to say that, as a nation, we need to create a new social role for the elderly. It is quite another to do something about the problem when your aging parent is pouting or acting out negative behavior right in your living room. But the first step to finding a solution is to address directly your parents' feelings about their own self-esteem.

You will hear me say time and again in this book, the key is communication. Once you understand the innocence behind their behavior, it will be easier for you to sit down and talk with your mom or dad about how they are feeling about themselves. If they say things such as "I'm bored" or "I don't know what to do with my time," you're lucky, because it gives you a great opportunity to help them help themselves into a solution.

An excellent response would be, "You've always said you wanted to . . ." and take it from there. Perhaps you could encourage your parent to write a short book about the experiences of her lifetime, encouraging her by relating how such a book would be important to her grandchildren and future generations. This is not made-up work for them. Sharing their heritage is an important role for the elderly and one they should take seriously.

This particular request, seriously made by my wife to her father after the prolonged illness and death of her mother, gave a healthy and intelligent elderly man a new zest for life and brought him out of a serious psychological decline. Dad has had a fascinating life as a missionary and spent many years in India. "Write about what our life was like back then," Betty requested. "It's the only way our children, your grandchildren, will have any idea of what it was really like." It took more encouragement from the whole family, but the payoff was amazing. Not only did Dad begin writing his memoirs and turn out a wonderful piece of personal family history, he also got a sparkle back in his eyes and a lift in his step. Not long ago, he met a lady twenty years his junior, and shortly after that remarried. Today, in his eighties, he is active, healthy, involved in life, and acts every bit the new bridegroom.

The approach Betty took was what I call *noninvasive intervention*. It is a gentle but firm persuasion that empowers an elderly person suffering from loss and depression to grab hold of life again instead of continuing a downhill slide. We will investigate this technique more fully in later chapters.

Another suggestion would be to encourage your elderly parent to become a volunteer. Most elderly people enjoy giving back to society, and the large number of elderly who volunteer in community organizations give testament to the satisfaction they find in doing so. Seniors who volunteer their time and services to others report a high level of satisfaction with their lives, while those who remain relatively isolated are the ones who complain of being unproductive.

It is on the volunteer front that I see the greatest opportunity to create a meaningful defined social role for the elders of our country. A volunteer force of the magnitude these people could provide would make a dramatic impact on our society. Chronically underfunded federal and private agencies could benefit from this rich source of talented, experienced manpower. Charitable institutions, hospitals, churches, youth organizations, schools and universities, city, county and state governments, correctional institutions, the armed services . . . the list of those who could use extra help for the good of us all goes on and on.

Although thousands of seniors are already deeply involved in volunteerism, many more could benefit from sharing their talents and experience by volunteering to help those who need their help. If we as a nation held the role of the volunteer in greater esteem, we could encourage even greater participation among the elderly and create for them a serious, defined role in our society. I would call them *Citizens Emeritus*, and the message is that we as a society venerate them and recognize their contributions. "Retired, but still valued," we would be telling them. At the same time, we would be opening an avenue for millions of older people to feel productive again and to repair their weakened self-esteem.

So encourage your complaining, irritable parent to get off the sofa and away from the TV and put herself to work again in a meaningful way. Even someone who is housebound because of physical disability may be able to participate in activities such as telephoning or stuffing envelopes. Your Area Agency on Aging can refer you and your parent to those organizations needing help.

Another thing we can do to overcome the problem of low self-esteem among the elderly is to change our own way of thinking about them. We need to drop the youth worship our society has indulged in since the arrival of the baby boom and eliminate the many negative stereotypes of aging that pervade our society. As the baby boomers themselves grow older, this probably will follow automatically, but the time to start is now. The time has come for Americans to venerate the elderly much as the Oriental cultures have always done. They have much to offer. We still have much to learn.

We need to redefine old age and encourage the "young old" to stay in the mainstream longer than they do. It is a fact that the longer a person stays active and involved in life, the less likely he or she is to suffer from many illnesses that plague our elderly today. The sixty-five-year-olds who think they have to retire are simply buying into one of the most stubborn stereotypes of aging we have created in this century. In the 1930s when the Social Security Administration established sixty-five as the age for receiving benefits, the fact was that most people did not live that long. Back then, sixty-five was "old old." Today, it is very "young old."

Health Care and Assisted Living Alternatives

Other specific issues need our attention if we are to relieve the stress on the Sandwich Generation and those elderly who must depend upon them. First, our health care delivery system needs an overhaul to provide quality care for the increasing numbers of elderly who will strain it to the breaking point in the coming years. Right now, only a little over ten percent of the population is over sixty-five years old, but this ten percent consumes over thirty-three percent of our health care resources. The cost of caring for them is disproportionately high because they must be treated for long-term chronic illnesses as opposed to the shorter-term acute illnesses suffered by the younger population.

Alternative living arrangements are going to be needed for this and upcoming elder generations. It is simply not realistic in many cases for families of the elderly to bring them into their homes for care. Lack of space, lack of finances, lack of time and energy by the caregiver are all good reasons to seek out alternatives to this solution. Another good reason is that, for the most part, elders prefer intimacy, but at a distance. Many will accept much needed help if it is not forced on them in close quarters. This intimacy at a distance is not possible if the generations are sharing the same household.

Unfortunately, in many areas, the only alternative available presently is the dreaded "old folks home," now known as a *skilled nursing facility* (SNF), which is not really an alternative at all unless the elderly need long-term critical nursing care. For those who need only some assistance, we must move quickly to design and develop affordable senior housing that allows the elderly to retain their autonomy and independence as much as possible and, at the same time, provides the assistance they need. These *adult congregate living facilities*, or ACLFs, have begun to spring up across the country in response to this need. If you have such assisted living residences in your area, pay each of them a visit and investigate the possibility of your aging parent relocating to one of them rather than into your home. If there is no such facility nearby, contact your city or county zoning board to see if anything is planned for the near future. If not, take the issue to the people through the media. Until a demand is known, the need may go unfulfilled.

As an individual, you can do many things to help both yourself and your aging parent resolve the dilemma in which you find yourselves. I suggest, as I did to Marge whom we met earlier in this chapter, that you learn as much as possible about the physiological, emotional, mental and behavioral changes that take place as we grow older. Educate yourself about your community's resources. You may be surprised at how much help is available in health care, transportation, volunteer opportunities for the elderly and respite for yourself.

Recognize that you are not alone. Find or form a support group of others who are faced with the same problems. Finally, try the techniques outlined in the following chapters. These are the ones I have found most effective in dealing with aging individuals.

There is much to be done, and the clock is ticking.

2

You Know

You've Got a Problem When . . .

Before you can do anything to help your elderly parent, you need to know that she is in need of help. Recognizing the signs is not always easy. Unfortunately, in our society, we often live many miles from our parents, and it is difficult to find the time and money to visit frequently. Consequently, many of us don't really know how Mom and Dad are getting along.

To make matters worse, many elderly people don't wish to be a burden on their children, so they don't let on when they are having a problem, or they deny that anything is wrong. They continue to try to cope with life although their physical strength and coping skills are insufficient. Talking to them on the phone, you may never know that your mother fell and twisted an ankle, or that your dad hasn't shaved in three days. It's not that they are ashamed of what happened or how they look; they just don't want you to know there is anything wrong. Besides not wanting to be a burden, many elderly people are afraid that if anyone found out they needed help it would mean having to move into an "old folks home," a specter worse than death to many.

Sometimes the situation is just the opposite. Some people never realize their parents really do need help because the parents have demanded their help so often in the past, no matter how trivial the need, that the children no longer pay much attention. These parents are guilty of crying wolf, often trying to make their children feel guilty for not visiting more often, reminding them in every phone call that they are getting older and they need more attention. If you have been prey to this kind of communication, you may not believe them when their cry for help is real. Sometimes it takes a call from someone who is physically near them to let you know that this time they aren't crying wolf.

If you are suspicious that things are not as they should be, and you cannot pay a visit to your parents in person, ask a close friend, neighbor or relative to look in on them and give you a call. However, urge them to be discreet about their mission, so as not to give your parents the feeling they are being spied upon. I call this *noninvasive intervention*, and I'll discuss this at greater length in later chapters.

If the report is that your parents are not doing so well coping with life, pack your bags and be on your way. The only way to solve a problem is to find out what it is. I strongly recommend that adult children with aging parents visit them as often as possible, making long-distance trips every six months, or at least once a year. You will be able to see immediately if their health, both physical and mental, is deteriorating. Such visits also provide excellent opportunities for intergenerational communication and planning, which are two primary keys to helping your elderly parents enjoy a high quality of life until the very end.

Senescence

Another reason it may be hard to recognize your parent's problems is the insidious nature of senescence, which is the increase in vulnerability that occurs with the frailty that comes with aging. Unlike an obvious crisis, such as a stroke, fall, or other calamity that gets your attention immediately, senescence has a way of sneaking up on us and the effects are not always dramatic or apparent on the surface.

I mentioned Dr. Hayflick's experimentation with cell replication in the last chapter. Besides discovering that our cells have a finite life span, Dr. Hayflick also showed how the cells begin to wear out before they completely give up. Although the functions of our bodies are considerably more complicated, for ease of understanding, compare what happens when our cells replicate again and again to what happens when a document is photocopied many times. As it is reproduced from one generation to another, it loses clarity until sometimes it becomes unreadable. So, too, our cells lose their strength or misreplicate after reproducing themselves many times.

As this happens, we begin to experience the effects of senescence, i.e., a dulling of the senses, a loss of muscle strength and tone, and a general loss of some reserve capacity of our vital organs. Our mental capacity to integrate information starts to diminish, and we cannot make decisions about as many things simultaneously as we once did.

Most of us experience the early effects of senescence as a series of small losses that we sort of learn to live with. If you are in your middle years and find you don't have the energy you once did, chances are you will try to find the right vitamin to give you more energy or embark on an exercise program guaranteed to take off excess weight and increase your energy. If you see some silver threads among the gold, you may find yourself perusing the hair color products at the drug store. These and other techniques are a younger person's way of coping with the early effects of senescence.

The elderly, who suffer much more pronounced effects, find it much more difficult to cope. For them it is not a matter of vitamins and hair dye. It can be a matter of having the energy to get out of bed in the morning. It can be the frustration of not being able to make decisions as easily and quickly as they once could, or not being able to make them at all.

Senescence robs us all, in time, of youthful vim and vigor. But no one can truly understand how it feels to be old until we get there. The best we can do, as younger caregivers to our elderly parents, is to be on the alert for signs that senescence is beginning to render their lives more difficult and to stand ready to help them in ways that work for both generations.

Signs of Senescence

One of the first signs that an elderly person is having trouble and may need some help is when he or she can no longer handle their own "ADLs," or *activities of daily living*. These are the things we all do daily to get through life —eating, toileting, bathing, dressing, keeping house—all those fundamentals of human existence (see table 2.1). The first clue you may have that a parent is having trouble coping with the effects of senescence is the neglect of one or more of these functions.

If you see that your father hasn't shaved in several days, especially if he has always been careful about his hygiene, it may be a sign that something is wrong. (It also may be a sign that he wants to grow a beard, so be careful.) If your mother needs a bath, or it is obvious that her clothing is soiled, you know you have a problem.

Noticeable weight loss is another dramatic clue. Often an older person becomes depressed and loses interest in food. Or, if dementia is a problem, he or she may forget to eat, or even how to eat, although if this is the problem, you will have noticed other signs by now. Malnourishment is a major cause of illness among the frail elderly, as is dehydration, which leads to toxicity from the multiple drugs many are using. When you visit your parents, look (discreetly) in the refrigerator and cupboards. Is there food in store? Is the kitchen clean? Are there signs of food preparation? Casually ask your parents about what they've had to eat lately. Try to evaluate if they are eating properly, or if at all.

TABLE 2.1
Activities of Daily Living (ADLs)

Ambulation	Toileting
Bathing	Transfer from toilet
Bowel and bladder control	Transfer from bed
Communication	Upper extremities (for example, grasping objects, picking up objects
Dressing	
Feeding	
Grooming	Visual acuity
Range of motion of limbs	

Their environment also will let you know how well they are coping with life. Unwashed laundry piled high, dishes stacked in the sink and washed only as they are needed, filth in the bathroom, soiled sheets all speak of people who can no longer handle the everyday chores of life.

Beyond the ADLs, you also should consider how well your parents are handling their "IADLs," or *instrumental activities of daily living*. These are chores that, although not basic life support activities like the ADLs, keep us all independently functioning in our society—things like balancing the checkbook, driving a car, staying in social contact with our friends, even dialing a telephone (see table 2.2). When your parent becomes unable to handle one or more of this kind of activity, it is time to find a way to fill in gently where she can no longer do the job.

TABLE 2.2
Instrumental Activities of Daily Living (IADLs)

Ability to perform in paid employment	Reading
Cleaning	Shopping
Climbing stairs	Traveling out of town
Cooking	Using public transportation
Laundry	Using telephone
Managing money	Walking outdoors
Managing medications	Writing
Outside work (for example, gardening, snow shoveling)	

Behavioral Changes

The most frightening changes you may see in your aging parent are not always physical. The elderly, for many reasons, often undergo dramatic changes in their behavior. Some of these stem from illness, others from depression, and a few, although a very small percentage, from true dementing illnesses such as Alzheimer's disease.

Perhaps one of the biggest fears of the elderly and the biggest threats to their children is the possibility of their becoming senile. We will take a closer look at this in the next chapter, but senility is one of those stubborn stereotypes of aging that generates much misinformation and misdiagnosis. Actually, I find the word "senile" often is used as an old-fashioned catchall for behavior that appears irrational, and it has no value as a medical diagnosis. The appropriate word for true mental confusion, at any age, is *dementia.*

One sign that your elderly mom needs help is mental confusion and forgetfulness. But just because she exhibits this behavior does not necessarily mean she is becoming senile. It may mean simply that senescence has diminished the capacity of her older brain to process as many thoughts simultaneously as it used to and to hold onto those thoughts in the memory bank.

There are ways to tell the difference between confusion and forgetfulness and true dementing illness, which we will investigate in the next chapter, but you must resist falling for the old stereotype that terrorizes us at the thought of our aging parent becoming senile. It is the perpetuation of the myth that most old people eventually become senile that cripples the spirit of the older generation and creates a type of *gerontophobia* among those who are charged with caring for the aged.

Substance Abuse

Behavioral changes in the elderly are quite common and can be caused by several things including substance abuse. As I mentioned above, senescence causes deterioration in the tissues of the body, including the vital organs whose job it is to process toxins, including drugs and alcohol. With senescence, the stomach, liver, intestines, and kidneys all diminish in capacity. An elderly person simply cannot tolerate the strength of drugs or alcohol they once could.

Over sixty percent of the elderly misuse the drugs they take, and they take a lot of drugs. Studies have shown that one-third of all prescription drugs are consumed by elderly people, some of whom may take from four to eight different pills a day for various problems. Sometimes doctors do not know that their patients are seeing other physicians, each prescribing medications for specific problems. Some of these drugs may not be compatible, causing dementia-like symptoms.

It is easy for the elderly to overdose on medications as well, even though they are taking the prescribed amount properly. Because of their slower metabolism, caused by senescence, they are at a greater risk of experiencing toxic effects from the drugs they ingest. The usual recommended adult dosage for most drugs was developed by the pharmaceutical companies for men 22 to 26 years old weighing 150 pounds. An eighty-year-old woman weighing one hundred and ten pounds cannot possibly process the same quantity of the medicine, and the result can be mental confusion, sickness or even death. The elderly very often may be unknowingly abusing the very drugs that are intended to help them!

Underdosing can be just as dangerous. Sometimes older people forget to take needed medication, or they deliberately refuse to take it because of its high cost or a belief that it is not really necessary. Sometimes they refuse to take the drugs they need because they perceive dependence on drugs as a bad thing or that medication use may imply to others that they have become sick. For whatever reason, an elderly person needs help if he or she is not taking medications properly.

If your parent is taking any medications, you should be aware of: (1) what kind, (2) how much, and (3) how often. Make sure all the physicians your parent is seeing know about each other and what medications have been prescribed. Make an appointment to visit your parent's primary care physician and share your knowledge of what medications she is taking. Ask if overmedication from these specific drugs could be the root of your parent's mental disorientation or bizarre behavior.

Another behavioral change that should send a loud warning signal that an elderly person needs help is related to alcohol consumption. It is estimated that ten to fifteen percent of the elderly are alcoholics. Some of them arrive at old age that way; others become alcoholic later in life. However, I often saw in nonalcoholic individuals abusive consumption of alcohol because of loneliness and withdrawal from depression. Yet, as with drugs, an older person's physical tolerance for alcohol is diminished. In a younger adult, the liver may be able to filter about one ounce of liquor in an hour. In an older person, that capacity may have diminished by as much as half. Without knowing it, the elderly person can spend much more time under the influence and may experience the changes in personality that afflict alcoholics. Alcohol also may be incompatible with medication, creating a stress on the older person's system resulting in erratic behavior and possibly symptoms of dementia.

Depression

Less easily recognizable, but a major threat to the health and well-being of elderly people is depression. Depression among the elderly is often triggered by a loss, real or perceived, and their subsequent inability to cope.

Loss comes in many forms to the elderly. It can be the loss of health, loss of financial security, loss of family and friends through death, or a general loss in the quality of their lives. The loss can be the realization that the funds so carefully saved to take care of the person's retirement have been seriously eroded by inflation. Although such a loss is not sudden, the effect is as devastating as if someone had actually robbed them.

Whatever the loss, the person becomes overwhelmed. Coping skills fail, and the person begins to withdraw. She begins to question her abilities, undermining her own feelings of self-worth. This leads to isolation, which in turn engenders depression, confused thinking, and physical self-neglect. What is worse, once it starts it is hard to stop the downward spiral: a person's confused thinking leads to a fear of being unable to cope, which in turn leads to further insecurities that cause the person to withdraw even more.

Depression masks itself in many ways. Some depressed people stop eating. Others eat all the time. Some start drinking. Some lose interest in doing anything at all. If you suspect your parent needs help but you can't pinpoint the problem, possibly she is in desperate need of treatment for severe depression.

There is much you can do to help your elderly loved one who may be displaying one or more of the signs of distress, and the first step is to get to the root of the problem. Here comes the "C" word again—communication. If possible, start by trying to get your parent to open up and share what is bothering her. Involve her in conversations where she has the opportunity, either directly or indirectly, to express her feelings, beliefs and opinions, and listen for the *feeling* behind the words that will help you understand her own separate reality. Don't try to second-guess your parent's thinking. What you may believe is the problem may not be a problem at all, and something you'd never suspect may be the real trouble. Listen, with as much patience as it takes, until you find out what is really going on with your aging parent.

Try to get your parent to make the decisions that will affect her life. One depressing aspect of aging is the fear of losing control over one's own affairs. If the elderly person can retain control over her own decision-making, it will be much easier to carry out the changes that will ultimately result in a higher quality of life.

Encourage your parent to have a complete physical exam every six months. If possible and appropriate, go along and see the doctor together. Be sure your parent is telling her doctor the whole story. Remember, if your parent is reluctant to tell you what's wrong, she's probably also not telling her doctor everything.

Above all, when you are poking around your parent's house and personal life, do it in a noninvasive way. Express your concerns, ask how you can help, but don't go in like a storm trooper. The elderly have feelings as fragile as their physiques. You will get much farther if you approach the situation in a way that allows her to retain her dignity and self-respect and to participate in her own problem-solving.

3

Don't Panic!

It's Christmastime. You haven't seen your mother since your father died last spring, and you're eagerly looking forward to spending the holidays with her. You know it's going to be tough on all of you this first year without Dad around, but you think that having the family together will make things easier for everyone.

But when you ring the doorbell and go inside the house, you know at once that something is wrong. Instead of greeting you with her normal, hearty hug, your mother shuffles toward you, clicking and fussing, saying she's been worried, you're so late. When you hug her, her body feels frail. Looking around, you notice things aren't as tidy as they used to be. There's no tree trimmed in the corner. There's no wood in the fireplace. And what's more alarming, there's no food in the house. "Couldn't be bothered," your mother snaps. "I knew you'd take care of it when you got here." Which is true, but it hurts when you hear her mumble under her breath, "Always comes in and takes right over. Don't know why I should bother. . ."

Not exactly the homecoming you expected, and your mother is not at all like the loving, independent woman she was this time last year. You blink back the tears that are stinging your eyes and swallow over the fear that's forming in the pit of your stomach. What's going on here? you scream inwardly, and you feel a sudden panic rising from deep within. Is Mom becoming senile?

It is frightening to visit an elderly parent after a prolonged absence and find your loved one is no longer mentally or physically sound. A natural knee-jerk reaction, based on our society's tendency to classify all erratic behavior in the elderly as senile, is to panic and cast a layman's diagnosis of senility on the situation. I have never found panic or an automatic, unfounded diagnosis to solve many problems. A better reaction is to rein in your emotions and, using this book as a guide, begin to examine the status quo. What IS going on here?

Besides the possible causes of a change in behavior in an elderly person outlined in the last chapter, there are other forces at work that may contribute to the problem. I would never venture to generalize too greatly about any group of people, but there are some common denominators in the psychological make-up of today's elderly which compound other problems.

A Coping Generation

Each generation faces its share of problems, but it seems the generation of those who are elderly today have had more than their fair share of disaster during their lifetimes——World War I, the Great Depression, World War

II, runaway inflation that eroded the buying power of their hard-earned dollars—these and other harsh political realities besides personal adversities. Theirs has been a lifetime of sacrifice and denial for the sake of family and country.

Whereas younger generations have had the good fortune to be able to focus on living well, the seniors of today were forced to cope so as to survive. To "cope" means "to struggle or contend, usually successfully." Today's elderly are skilled copers, so skilled that many of them have developed a coping mentality, a defensive, often inflexible reaction to the world that threatens them. It is their way of keeping their dukes up to defend themselves from adversity. They trust few, because so many have let them down. They are self-reliant, not wishing to expose themselves to the vulnerability that comes with depending on others.

Not surprisingly, many older people, despite their frailty, have carried this coping mentality into their old age as a defense against still another unexpected challenge life has handed them—living to be very, very old. They remain skeptical, wary, and fiercely independent, traits which, though admirable in some ways, often work against their best interests.

This defensive behavior often intensifies as the elderly person becomes more frail and feels more vulnerable. Afraid of losing control over her life, an elderly person may become suspicious, distrustful, somewhat paranoid, and even downright nasty to deal with. This behavior may stem from the physical and psychological problems mentioned above, but it also may be in part an attempt to cope with the rigors of growing old.

Unfortunately, it seems that sometimes their worst behavior is directed at those who least deserve it—a loving family member who is only trying to help. I hope I can show you there is innocence in this behavior. You have to understand what lies behind it and to find the courage and patience to cope with it yourself.

Another way many elderly people cope with the aging process is by living in the past. When a person reaches the later years, it can be frightening to look ahead down life's path. Whereas younger people can look forward to things getting better in the future, older people do not have the luxury of time on their side to improve their lot. So instead of looking forward and making better things happen in their old age, they cope by looking backward.

An older friend explained: "When I look back, my past seems like a very long road, but when I look forward, the road seems shorter than my driveway." My friend spends a lot of time reminiscing about the times in her life when she was happy and fulfilled, grieving the loss of the "good old days."

Often this happens when a person retires and finds her expectations of retirement fall short of her reality. In her younger years, she sublimated her desire to pursue interesting avocations because the work ethic was so rigid she needed constantly to reaffirm she was being productive. She coped with the frustrations of life by fantasizing about these exciting avocations she was going to pursue when she retired and had the time. But upon retirement, she finds those long-dreamed-of activities unfulfilling or only of short-term interest. She still faces frustrations with life, but no longer has her fantasy of the future as a coping mechanism, so she begins to cope by living in the past. Instead of establishing a "presence in the present" and finding new meaningful activities that would lead to a fulfilling life, she indulges in the dead-end thinking that comes with reminiscing and commiserating about the past.

Living in the past can lead to frustration, depression, anger, physical deterioration, and the destruction of previously harmonious relationships. It can erode self-esteem and destroy creativity. It is a very dangerous method of coping.

When Coping Skills Fail

Defensive behavior, living in the past, whatever coping mechanisms a person has been using may fail as the effects of senescence increase. With reserves of energy and vitality diminished, an elderly person often begins to doubt her ability to handle her own affairs and make decisions for herself. Life seems suddenly overwhelming, too big to handle—threatening. So now, in order to cope, the person simply begins to shrink her world down to a size she can manage. She becomes more purposeful in her activities, cutting out those things that create too much stress for her to deal with.

For example, a newly widowed resident in one of my retirement homes found that she was extremely uncomfortable being a single woman in a social setting with other couples. To cope, she simply isolated herself. She no longer went to the dances and potluck dinners. She quit participating in the many activities available at the community. Instead, she spent her time watching TV or simply sitting, doing nothing. She coped by sizing her world down to what she felt she could handle.

At first glance, this reaction seems to make sense. If you can't handle it, don't do it. However, when a person stops participating in life, it starts a dangerous downhill cycle that is hard to overcome. First, it fosters physical degeneration. When a person withdraws and becomes inactive and isolated, her body no longer gets the exercise it needs. She becomes vulnerable to both acute and chronic illness and other physical problems such as weakened muscles, stiff and aching joints, skin disorders, and very sluggish bowels. The physical deterioration alone contributes mightily to the downward spiral—the worse you feel, the less you do.

Coincidental with this, because she has little or no social contact to provide mental stimulation, an elderly person in this circumstance will likely become mentally dull as well. Often such a person will exhibit behavior that resembles dementia, such as forgetfulness, disorientation and mental confusion. To outsiders, it appears as if the old woman has finally become senile when that is simply not true. Rather, she has become a victim of what I call *circumstantial senility*.

Circumstantial Senility

Circumstantial senility is a phenomenon in which an elderly person intermittently exhibits the classic symptoms of true dementia though there is no physical reason for this behavior. It happens usually when the person chooses, either consciously or subconsciously, to withdraw from the circumstances of her life that seem too much with which to cope. Such a person usually suffers from low self-esteem and has started to doubt her ability to handle the affairs of her life and to make decisions on her own. This self-doubt leads to an even deeper erosion of self-confidence, making it more difficult to integrate enough thoughts to cope with problem-solving and decision-making. Eventually, this process spirals downward until the person is no longer able to make any decisions at all. Not only can she not decide what to have for dinner, she may not be able to decide whether to eat at all.

As a result, she may become malnourished. Needed medication may not be taken or dosage duplicated. Often personal hygiene is neglected, and illnesses go untreated. The person becomes prone to illness, accident and victimization, which leads to problems of even greater magnitude than the initial stress that started these down-hill wheels in motion. Unless someone intervenes to turn the situation around, the person eventually is likely to cope with these overwhelming circumstances simply by going to bed. The result of this downhill cycle is death, but only after a prolonged period of morbidity.

It is a sad fact that between five and fifteen percent of people over sixty-five in this country are in a complete mental shutdown, suffering from circumstantial senility at one level or another. It is especially deplorable when we know that with the right intervention and support, circumstantial senility is almost always reversible.

Dementia: What It Really Is

Before looking at how you can help an aging loved one get out of the downward spiral that leads to circumstantial senility, let me take a moment to describe true *dementia*. The word "dementia" comes from the Latin prefix "de" meaning "from" or "off" and the Latin word "mentis" meaning "the mind." Dementia itself is not a disease, but a description of *symptoms* caused by several different diseases. Dementias come in many forms and degrees. Some dementias are progressive and irreversible; others are quite treatable if diagnosed properly and in time.

The most important thing to remember about dementia is this:

LESS THAN SEVEN PERCENT OF ALL
PEOPLE OVER THE AGE OF SIXTY-FIVE
SUFFER FROM ANY FORM OF TRUE
DEMENTIA.

This means that most people die with their mental faculties intact after living long and vigorous lives. But the stereotype of senility prevails, and because of it, incredible numbers of elderly who display some symptoms of dementia never receive the proper treatment, for many people do not know that there are both irreversible and reversible dementing diseases.

The Reversible Dementias

The symptoms of dementia are mental confusion, forgetfulness, disorientation, and intellectual decline. All these can be caused by several very different things, including true dementing illnesses such as Alzheimer's disease, multi-infarct dementia, and the much rarer brain disorders. However, symptoms that mimic true dementia also may show up in the older patient who suffers from treatable illnesses. In fact, one main cause of the symptoms of dementia is physiological disease. Diabetes, hydrocephalus, infections, high blood pressure, arteriosclerosis, hormone imbalance, pituitary insufficiency, vascular disorders, and many other illnesses common among older people can create temporary mental confusion, making them appear senile.

Why do these things affect older people in this way and not younger? With senescence the brain, just as the other vital organs, loses some of its reserve capacity and is not able to handle the demands made upon it during illness. We are metabolically less able to function during a metabolic imbalance. When an elderly person catches a cold or the flu, for example, it not only makes their joints and muscles ache, their eyes burn, and their skin sensitive, it also affects the brain itself, decreasing its capacity still further. An elderly person with such an acute infection may become disoriented, hallucinatory, even temporarily amnesiac in extreme cases.

In addition to illness, conditions such as malnourishment, dehydration, anemia and vitamin deficiencies can all create demented behavior in older adults, and the aged are prone to dietary habits that can lead to all these. When an aging parent shows signs of dementia, among the first things you should look at is her diet.

I have already described the effects that medication can have on elderly people. Overdosing and mixing incompatible drugs and the intake of too much alcohol can all cause the symptoms of dementia.

The Irreversible Dementias

There are, unfortunately, also true dementing illnesses. Alzheimer's disease receives the biggest play in the media these days. To date no cure has been found, and as the population of elderly continues to expand, caring for Alzheimer's patients is going to become an increasing concern.

Alzheimer's is a disease, not a natural result of aging. Alzheimer's is a deterioration of the brain, which results in chronic loss of memory and personality changes. The cause of Alzheimer's is unknown. Some researchers have suggested that it might be viral in nature, while others favor the theory that it is caused by the accumulation of heavy metals, such as aluminum, in the brain. Still others are looking at biochemical imbalances as the source for the debilitating disease. It is not yet known whether the disease is hereditary, although there is mounting evidence that points to chromosomal or other genetic factors as the cause.

Autopsy is presently the only way to achieve a true diagnosis of Alzheimer's. Two changes are noted in the makeup of the brain in nearly all Alzheimer's victims, changes called "tangles" and "plaques." These abnormalities of the brain tissue occur most often in the regions of the brain associated with memory and intellectual functioning.

There is no known cure for Alzheimer's disease. It is a progressive illness that robs its victims of the ability to think, reason, and function in everyday life. Alzheimer's patients usually do not die of the disease itself, but rather from the side effects of the immobility it causes, such as infection, malnutrition, or a stroke.

Another form of true dementia strikes the next largest group of people. It is *multi-infarct dementia*, once called "hardening of the arteries of the brain." This dementia is caused by a series of little strokes within the brain. Individually, these strokes may not even be noticeable to the victim or those around her but, together, they can cause a loss of blood flow to the brain and a resultant loss of function in those regions where the ministrokes occur.

People suffering from multi-infarct dementia usually have a history of hypertension, strokes and blackouts. As with Alzheimer's, victims of multi-infarct dementia will never fully recover, although in some cases, rehabilitation can help restore function. Encouraging new medical findings reveal that, with proper training, control of certain functions and activities can be directed by another, undamaged, region of the brain.

Multi-infarct dementia usually progresses in a series of steps, in contrast to the gradual decline of Alzheimer's. A person may appear to stabilize after a noticeable decline, and then go for some time, even years, before suffering another setback. Each time the victim suffers a stroke, however, no matter how small, there is some death of brain tissue.

There are several mostly rare diseases that strike the brain resulting in irreversible dementia. Those afflicted are not necessarily restricted to the elderly, but when these diseases do strike an older person, it is important that they be diagnosed properly and not just sloughed off as senility. These include Huntington's disease, Creutzfeldt-Jakob disease, Pick's disease, Parkinson's disease, Friedreich's ataxia, progressive supranuclear palsy, Wilson's disease, Korsakoff's psychosis, kuru, and dementia pugilistica.

As you can see, with all these possibilities, it is critical that a confused, disoriented elderly person receive a careful, thoughtful diagnosis by her physician rather than being assumed to be senile. Unfortunately, the myth that dementia is natural to the aging process has pervaded the medical community as well, and often, doctors may not perform all the tests that might be necessary to learn whether the aging patient suffers from true dementia or another, treatable disease.

It is your responsibility as a loving, concerned daughter or son to make sure all avenues are explored before panicking and declaring your aging parent to be senile.

4

There Are Solutions

If you suspect or have already discerned your aging parent needs help, you must have the courage to take the steps necessary to see her situation turned around. First, you must do everything in your power to intervene in a noninvasive way to see that your parent receives an accurate and proper medical evaluation. Second, you need to find a way to open the lines of communication between your two generations. Third, you must empower your parent to begin the process of *countertransference*, a technique which will enable her to transfer some or most of her needs into your care, while maintaining control of much of her decision-making process and keeping her dignity intact.

Life Enhancement Intervention

I have called for noninvasive intervention from the daughters and sons of the elderly in need of help. To many, these terms seem in opposition; anytime anyone intervenes in someone else's affairs they also would be invading that person's privacy. The word "intervention" here, I think, is often confused with "interference." I am not calling on you to interfere, which connotes taking over. I am urging you instead to gently "knock on the door" and urge your parents them to allow you to help. I call this "Life Enhancement Intervention."

When senescence begins to steal away an elderly person's energy and ability to handle her own affairs, a natural reaction is for the person to withdraw from activities she can no longer cope with. Unless someone intervenes and stops the decline, a downhill pattern begins that can lead the elderly person into an extended phase of morbidity which ultimately results in death.

In the retirement facilities in which I have been involved, I have instituted a program that has as its goal the return of a person caught in this decline to proactive functioning, that is, to bring her out of circumstantial senility and return her to a level of functioning at which she can cope. To accomplish this, someone must intervene (see fig. 4.1).

As I have said before, a good first step is for you to visit your parent's primary care physician. This is what Marge was doing when she showed up at my office, although then, her sanity was more at stake than her mother's. In the following hour, we went over all of her mother's medical history, as well as her personal history and behavior patterns, both before she fell and after. We both learned a lot, and it opened a vital line of communication between us. Since she was her mother's primary informal caregiver and I the primary care physician, it was very important that we both be "watching the same movie." Each must know what the other is doing so as to be the most effective. Together we organized an orderly investigation into her mother's change in behavior, starting first with a complete medical checkup.

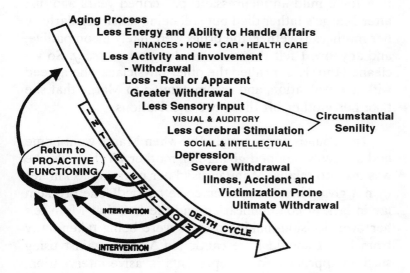

Fig 4.1. Proactive intervention and the aging process.

I wish to emphasize here how important it is for the elderly to receive an evaluation every six months. Senescence, the aging process, sometimes progresses quickly, and the only way to stay abreast of an elderly person's health is to monitor it frequently.

Before making her visit to my office, Marge had compiled a list of all the medications her mother was taking, including aspirin and other over-the-counter drugs. She also listed other specialists her mother had seen in the past two years, and the medications they had prescribed. After completing her physical, I reviewed the drugs and found two of them no longer necessary for her treatment. (Often, the elderly are so used to taking their pills every day, they no longer see them as drugs.) One was a pain-killer used at the time of her fall; the other was a prescription for a mild antidepressant, prescribed years ago just after Marge's father died but still being taken regularly by her mother. Together, the drugs were likely incompatible, and anyhow, I felt they were no longer necessary. So we cleaned the slate. I called the other physicians who agreed with my evaluation, and recommended to Marge that she take her mother off these two medications.

This sounds easy enough. But when Marge went home and suddenly stopped giving her mother all the pills she was used to taking, Mom accused her of trying to kill her by not giving her the medicine she needed! The problem lay in lack of communication and the fact that Mom felt her own decision-making powers were being taken away from her. I should have cautioned Marge against using such an approach, for it represents invasive intervention, no matter how innocent the intent. Mom was the patient, not Marge, and if the patient can mentally participate in her own care program, she should be allowed to do so. It is okay, and often even preferable, to make the first visit to the primary care physician by yourself. When it comes time to make decisions, such as withholding medications your parent is used to taking, include Mom in the office visit and the discussions with her doctor. Just because she has been showing signs of erratic behavior doesn't mean she can't or won't understand that this is being done for her better health. Such doctor's orders are more likely to be followed if they come directly from the doctor and not secondhand from you. This way, she won't perceive her independence and decision-making abilities are being threatened, and she will appreciate being allowed to retain that dignity.

To resolve this conflict between Marge and her mother, they came together to my office, where I explained to her mother in intellectual, adult terms that although her health seemed fine and that her hip had healed nicely, the medications she was taking were likely making her feel strange and off-balance. I described how the drugs worked against each other and against her system, and once she understood what was going on, she was happy to get rid of them. It was a beautiful first step in reopening the communication between Marge and her mother, a communication that had gotten lost in the crisis of her mother's fall and the consequent loss of her independence on being moved in with Marge's family. It was also a successful example of the way Life Enhancement Intervention works.

Communication: The Great Healer

Open communication, no matter how difficult at first, is the Great Healer of all types of problems for it allows you to put in place at least a social support system. Often when communication between elderly parents and their adult children is established concerning the care of the older generation, old misunderstandings and emotional wounds are also healed. Forgiveness for old transgressions from either side results, and both generations experience the warmth of being reunited emotionally with one another.

But how do you go about opening those vital lines of communication? Years and miles may have separated you from your parent, as well as those old, unresolved disagreements. Further, role reversal is often too painful and too emotional for the elderly to want to deal with. It would be unrealistic to think you can put aside such distance simply by saying, "Can we talk?" You must realize several things. First, it's up to you to take the first step. Don't expect your parent to come to you. For all the reasons we have already discussed—not wanting to be a burden, not wanting to lose control of her life or independence, defensive behavior, or just the inability to think clearly—it is rare that the elderly parent opens the communication.

Second, it takes time. Don't rush things, and don't think it's going to be easy. A person who has been used to handling her own affairs, being self-sufficient, and needing no outside help for seven or eight decades will be reluctant to even talk about changing the status quo. Feeling threatened and vulnerable, your elderly parent needs to know you are not trying to take over her life. So go slowly and allow time for a comfort level to be established firmly enough so that communication will truly be open and honest and countertransference can occur.

Finally, communication blossoms best in an atmosphere of unconditional love. No matter what has transpired between you and your parent, let her know you love her. Release old grudges and don't take on any new ones. Offer your help in terms of love and understanding of her feelings. Let her know you respect her intelligence, wisdom, and ability. In doing so, you will shore up her eroding self-esteem and restore her dignity, and in return she will feel secure and free to express not only her threatening insecurity but her love for you as well.

Just as you are most effective as parents when you treat your children with respect, so will you be with your elderly parents. Always let your communication with your elderly mother or father be based on mutual respect. Never, ever, talk down to them, no matter how childish their behavior may seem at times. Express your concerns without emotional embellishment. Say: "Mom, I'm concerned that you have lost weight since the last time I was here," rather than "You're skin and bones. Guess I'd better get in the kitchen and make you a decent meal." The first example opens the door for your parent to tell you what is wrong; the second accuses her of not being able to take care of herself any more. Although this may be true, going about it in this manner will only trigger defensive behavior, and you've lost a chance to get her on your side.

Always tell your parent of your belief in her ability to make positive changes that will improve her situation. She actually may be unable to take the action to carry out those changes, but the important thing is she can make the decision to make those changes. The rest may be up to you, but as long as you can assure her she holds the decision-making power, you diffuse any threat she may feel that you are taking away her autonomy. Remember Marge's mother's reaction when she wasn't included in the decision-making concerning her medication?

Many decisions your parent will likely have to make will involve the transference of some responsibilities for different areas of her life to you or other individuals. If some assistance with her ADLs or IADLs would help Mom enjoy a greater quality of life, you should help her make the decision to transfer some of these responsibilities into the hands of another. By doing so, she will be able to shrink her world to a size with which she can cope without triggering the withdrawal that leads to circumstantial senility. It is a very effective transaction, but it is also tricky for both generations.

Transference and Countertransference

From the moment we are born, our parents begin to teach us the ways of the world, initiating a process called *transference*. By sharing their knowledge and experience with us, they prepare us to become autonomous adults. As we become capable, they transfer the responsibilities of daily living to us to handle for ourselves. As soon as we can hold a spoon, the responsibility for feeding ourselves is transferred to us. When we learn to control our elimination, we assume those responsibilities, and our parents no longer have to change diapers. (Probably the most welcomed transference in the parenting experience!) When we learn to tie our shoes, it becomes our job to do so. This transference process is as natural as a mother bird pushing the baby bird out of the nest.

Perhaps the most difficult transference in the early part of our lives comes in our teenage years. When we reach this turbulent age, we want to become independent as quickly as possible, and yet we are unprepared for total independence. Parents are often confused, not knowing exactly how much responsibility a child can handle and when to let him have it. It is a source of serious conflict in many families.

Gradually, however, we complete the process, move out on our own, and assume full responsibility for our own

lives. Not long afterward, we begin the process of transference with our own children. We assume the role of
trainer and begin the transference of basic life skills to
our children, who one day, too, will leave the nest as fully
functioning adults.

Around this same time in our lives, our middle years,
many of us experience a much more challenging type of
transference, really a *countertransference*, a reversal in
roles, when our aging parents begin to transfer some
responsibilities for their care over to us. Throughout our
lives as human beings in a civilized society, we practice a
reciprocal support system by which the members of the
family with the best health and strongest resources assume
responsibility for providing material, emotional and social
support for others in the family. In our childhood years,
our parents provide this support for us. When our parents
grow old and frail, they often look to us to provide this
support for them. It is when they begin to need our
support to cope with senescence that countertransference
begins.

There is a significant difference between our transference experiences both as children and with children and
our countertransference experience with our parents. In
the earlier transference, one party, the parent, is in control
and calls the shots. But by the time our parents begin
countertransference to us, we usually have developed an
adult-to-adult relationship with them. They are not people
we have control over or can tell what to do. We relate to
them more as friends than as parents. Most often there
is idea exchange between adult children and their parents,
with parents sometimes even asking for advice from their
children. With open communication in a friendly relation-

ship, the difficulties that are inherent in countertransference can be greatly reduced, but make no mistake, this phase of life can be just as stormy as the teenage years.

There is also a profound emotional difference between transference and countertransference. The early transference is usually a positive experience for both parents and children because it signals the maturing of the younger generation into fully autonomous, independent individuals. Countertransference, on the other hand, can represent a loss of autonomy for the older generation, many of whom are becoming progressively more dependent on their children to meet their needs. When this happens, there is a recognition on both sides, usually unspoken, that life for that aging loved one no longer holds the quality it once did. In spite of whatever differences we may have with our elderly parents or whatever ambivalence we may feel at being burdened with caring for them, we also usually venerate our aged loved ones. They have much to share with us and their grandchildren, and it saddens us to see them losing their strength and vigor.

Countertransference is difficult for the Sandwich Generation who must deal not only with the emotional stress of seeing an elderly loved one decline but who also may be faced with trying to find time, money, and energy to accept the burdens being transferred back to them. If you are busy trying to help a teenager through his or her own transference process in growing up, plus trying to balance career and home responsibilities, the added burden of meeting some or all of your aging parents' needs may be more than you feel you can cope with.

It is not uncommon for people like you to feel strongly ambivalent toward your aging parents. On the one hand, you want to help and do what is best for them, but on the other, the stress it imposes on your life leaves you physically and emotionally drained. There doesn't seem enough of you to go around, and sometimes you find it difficult to feel loving toward your parents because you are so angry at the situation. Sound familiar?

But the Sandwich Generation is not the only group to experience anger and frustration at the time of counter-transference. When your aging parents come face-to-face with the fact they can no longer remain independent and self-supporting, it may very well be the most traumatic moment in their lives. Feeling their independence and autonomy threatened can bring all kinds of monsters out of their emotional closets, from fear, depression and hopelessness to anger, frustration and aggressive behavior. And when it is their children who are suggesting that they give up some of their independence, they may feel resentment and hostility, sometimes believing the children are just a little too eager to put them out to pasture. For persons who have been active and in control of things all of their lives, this experience can be humiliating and denigrating, although it may be the result of good intentions by the younger generation.

Caregiver Prejudice

There is still another phenomenon that can snarl your attempts at helping your parents through a smooth countertransference. I call it *caregiver prejudice*. Often, elderly people are receiving care from someone other than their own children, especially while they are still able to cope fairly well with their lives as they age. They may live with another elderly person such as a brother or sister. Perhaps a good friend who lives next door watches out for them, or they may rely on members of their church to stop in and provide small amounts of support.

These informal caregivers are usually also good friends, and there is a good deal of bonding between them. As the years go by, the caregivers/friends may become infirm themselves, or the children may witness a deterioration in their elderly parents' conditions that motivates them to take over the caregiving role, sometimes with little regard for the feelings of the other people involved. This is a form of invasive intervention, and both the elderly persons and the previous caregiver may resent the intrusion and resist the imposed change. The "where-were-they-when-you-needed-them-before?" syndrome can rear its ugly head, and hurt feelings may turn into outright hostility. Sometimes the caregiver who is pushed aside projects her experiences into the situation and begins to prejudice the elderly person against her family.

For example, one of Marge's mother's problems when Marge insisted she move in with her family was that Mom's best friend from church didn't approve of the move. Now, this friend had become an informal caregiver to Mom over the past two years, and being an older person herself and sharing the same fears of loss of autonomy, she continued to call Mom up and fill her ears with her own prejudice concerning Mom's living arrangements.

Older people are especially vulnerable to this kind of manipulation when they make their initial countertransference to the wrong individual, and it leaves them exposed to unethical people who prey on their insecurities. Hired companions, for example, can take horrible advantage of those persons with whose care they are charged.

Caregiver prejudice makes it even more difficult for the children of aging parents to help them affect countertransference that is appropriate and in their best interest. If your aging parent has formerly established a close relationship with such a person, be aware of this phenomenon and be prepared to deal with it positively, in a way that both your parent and the former informal caregiver can accept.

It's not an easy task you face, is it? Intervene, but don't interfere. Put up with behavior that in your own children you would reprimand. Communicate, even if your parent resists. Love unconditionally. Help create countertransference even when you may feel on overload yourself. Deal positively with disapproving friends.

No, it's not an easy task. But have the courage to stick with it through these tough times and you might very well find the results will release you from a self-imposed bondage and change your life in a very positive way. You may find it one of the most rewarding things you've ever done. Keep reading for some ideas to help you along the way.

Working Out Plans Together

The best time to resolve the question "What shall we do about Mom?"is *before* any crisis arises, when both you and your aging parents can communicate on equal footing and make plans together for possible eventualities. I cannot stress strongly enough that planning ahead is the most effective way to assure a smooth countertransference and avoid the problems inherent in crisis decision-making. Advanced planning takes the emotional reaction out of difficult decisions and allows objective thinking to plan right action instead. Like the old Boy Scout motto says, it's wise to "Be Prepared."

Unfortunately, too few people actually do much, if any, advanced planning for the time when they're too frail to care for themselves. They plan for their death better than they plan for their life. Many older Americans, no matter their degree of wealth, have some form of will in place, perhaps some life insurance to help cover their final expenses. Some even go to the extent of purchasing burial plots and paying in advance for their funerals. Many aging parents will alert their adult children to the location of their will and insurance policies, "just in case." Not many, however, call a family meeting and say, "Let's make some decisions now so we'll all be ready if the time ever comes that Mom and I need help."

Advanced planning for countertransference, living arrangements, and personal care could save many hurt feelings, avoid much anger, and result in both the elderly and the Sandwich Generation enjoying a higher quality of life. However, all too often, it takes a crisis to shake us up enough to think about the "what ifs." The death of one of your parents, a critical illness or accident, or even just the sudden shocking recognition on your part that your elderly parent needs help can trigger intergenerational planning, but unfortunately, by this time, decision-making can't help but be affected by the crisis environment.

But you have to start somewhere, and if it takes a crisis to bring a family to the realization that some planning is in order, it's better than operating with no planning at all. Getting back to Marge's case, the family missed one opportunity to make advanced plans together when her father died. Yes, it was a time of crisis, but if they had thought then to look ahead at what the future might hold for the widowed mother, all of the family could have recognized the time had come to make some plans together. At the time, however, Marge's mother was strong and healthy and after her initial grief, began to function quite well on her own again. It was only when a second crisis hit, when Mom fell and injured her hip, that the absence of advanced planning took its toll.

Postcrisis planning is possible, but it is much more difficult because both generations are feeling the stress of being thrust unexpectedly into unpleasant circumstances. It wasn't until the pressure almost sent Marge over the edge that she sought help and finally began to work out a plan with her mother that enhanced both their lives.

Opening a Dialogue

Just how do you get such planning under way? You must find a way to open a dialogue with your elderly parents. In Marge's case, that dialogue started in my office when she and her mother came back together to work out the issue of her mother's medication. Once her mother understood Marge's motivations and even her extreme stress, the two began communicating in earnest to find a way to resolve their problems.

You must somehow get your parent to start thinking about the future, even if it does look "shorter than the driveway." Although reminiscing can be constructive and helpful, living in the past is no good and ignoring the future is even worse. Find a quiet time and place when your parent is rested and at ease and play the "what if" game. Ask, "What if you become ill and can't live alone? What would you want me to do?" Or, "What if you had a stroke and lost your voice. If you couldn't talk, how could we communicate so I would know what your wishes are?" Or, "What if you fell and broke your hip and needed to spend some rehabilitation time in a convalescent home. Do you think it would be possible for us to visit some and see which we like the best, just in case?"

The "what if" approach works well because it de-emotionalizes the issues and asks your parent to express her wants. It shows you respect her ability to make decisions about her own future and that you wish to facilitate her requests.

Whatever response you get, negative or positive, validate the answer. For example, if your Mom says, "I wish I'd just die and get it over with," respond by saying something like, "I can understand why you feel that way. You've certainly had your share of tough times lately." Then grow quiet and see what comes next. The reality is that your Mom most likely doesn't really want to die and get it over with, but your answer will likely take her by surprise. Instead of trying to talk her out of her negative thinking, which puts you in charge, you are validating her feelings, and by that keeping her in charge. She may respond with a typical coping answer such as: "Oh, it really hasn't been all that bad," showing you she still is able to handle things in spite of setbacks. It is important in all conversations you have with your elderly parents that they know you are not trying to wrest control of their lives from them, but rather to empower them through your help and support to stay in control, in a way that works better for them than what is going on presently.

One technique that is quite effective in getting an elderly person to start thinking about the future again and to consider making some plans with you is to restate that person's answers as questions, thereby encouraging further exploration of the person's inner feelings, fears, and wants. If your parent says "I just don't want to go to the old folks home," ask "You don't want to go to the old folks home?" I know that sounds silly and redundant, but it works. Keeping your mouth shut also works. Give your parent time to respond. "No. Those places are for old folks who just sit around waiting to die," would be a likely reply in this conversation. Your response: "That doesn't sound like much fun." Then ask, "What would you rather do instead?"

Parent: "I'd rather . . . I'd rather it would be like it used to be."

You: "You'd rather it would be like it used to be? When?"

Parent: "When your dad and I first married. We used to have the greatest times."

You: "You used to have the greatest times? Doing what?"

Parent: "Oh, just being together, you know, doing things together."

You: "What did you do?"

Parent: "We used to go to the beach and get ice cream on the boardwalk. Oh, those were the days. . . ."

Now, don't allow this conversation to slip into just a reminiscence about the past, which then could lead to commiseration about the present. Instead, guide it gently by saying, "I know how much you and Dad liked to go for ice cream. Did you know there's a new ice cream parlor at the shopping center?" This brings the thoughts back to the present, but in a pleasant context that validates your parent's fond memories. Then continue to ask questions based on your parent's responses until you begin to get at the core of the problem.

What you are doing when you validate your parent's comments is also validating her worth as a human being. Often the frustrations experienced by the elderly stem from a feeling of being unproductive, even to the extent of feeling useless. The point in using the "what if" game and having this kind of conversation at all is to get your parents to understand how important they are to you and your family and that their lives still have great worth and dignity. You are also empowering them to talk about what is bothering them and to be involved in the decision-making process.

The success of your efforts may depend a great deal on the physical surroundings in which you begin to broach the subject. As I said, find a quiet time when your parent is rested, and make sure that she is comfortable. Don't underestimate the power of nonverbal communication—physical closeness works well in breaking down barriers. If you feel comfortable doing so, sit side-by-side on a sofa or love seat. Take your parent's hand and give it a loving squeeze. Or touch a cheek. Smile. Say I love you, both in words and in gestures. Allow yourself to open up. It will make it easier for your parent to do so as well. Enjoying a cup of tea, hot chocolate, or other favorite treat also helps establish a positive and cooperative mood.

Speak calmly. Make sure you yourself are centered before beginning. If your emotions aren't stabilized, you will subconsciously communicate your distress and panic to your parent, which will usually generate reciprocal emotions. Keep your own feelings to yourself. This is your time to listen. Your time to learn.

Listen for the Feeling

When your parent begins to open up to you, the words and the feelings expressed may be two different things. Listen to the words, for sure, but pay particular attention to the feelings behind them. When your mother says: "I don't need your help. I don't want to be a burden on you," she may really be saying, "Yes, I do need help, but I am afraid of losing my independence." At age fifty-five, eighty-six percent say they need no help, but by age seventy-five, seventy-two percent look to their children for assistance.

Using the technique described above, dig for more feelings. "You don't want my help because you're afraid you'll be a burden?" Her answer might be: "Yes. I've always been able to take care of myself." Here the feelings are beginning to surface. Try again. "I know you've always been self-sufficient. It's something I've always admired in you." From here, the conversation might go like this:

Mom: "Yes. I've always wanted to be independent. Even when your dad was alive, I liked being able to do for myself."
You: "Is that why you started your knit shop?"
Mom: "It sure is. Not that I didn't need your father, you understand, but just because. . . ."
You: "Because you needed to know you could stand on your own if you had to?"
Mom: "Yes, I guess that was it. And I'm no different now than I was then. I still want to stand on my own."
You: "Are you afraid if I help you, that you will lose some of that independence you worked so hard for?"
Mom: "Yes, I guess that's so."

Because you have listened for the feeling behind the words, you have now successfully gotten to the meat of the subject, the fear of losing independence and self-sufficiency that then yields insecurity which in turn results in behavior that is easily misunderstood. You have made major progress, because she has finally acknowledged her fears out loud. It is quite likely that until now, even she did not know exactly what her resistance was to your offers of help.

The moment is prime for you to validate not only her fears but also her worth as a valuable human being. Reply: "I can understand how you feel. You always have been a real source of strength to everybody in the family, and you know what? You still are!" This followed by silence, or better yet a hug, opens the door even wider.

Address the Issues Intellectually

Although this can be a highly emotional scenario, if you try to address the issues from an intellectual standpoint rather than an emotional one, you establish a safe zone of communication. Instead of making the points too personal and possibly too uncomfortable for the older person, you will be making them more in the abstract, and therefore not as threatening. In other words, make this discussion generic. Also by doing this, you validate your parent's intelligence and show your respect for her ability to control her life.

Start by explaining the idea of countertransference. Don't compare your parents' need to make transference to the transference experience with parenting, because no elderly person likes to be compared to a child. Just explain that in all societies, families practice the reciprocal support system I mentioned in the last chapter. Those with the strongest resources, whether it be health, energy or money, help those with fewer resources. It is the natural order of life. Then point out quickly that accepting a little help here and there does not mean giving up one's independence. It simply means transferring some of those things that are taxing and trying for one person to another who has more coping resources to deal with them. In this way, energy is often freed up and the person can enjoy life again.

It is very important for both generations to realize that countertransference does not happen all at once. It is incremental and accomplished only as needed. Your mother may only need help with one or two ADLs, activities of daily living, to make a big difference in her life. There is no reason for her to turn over responsibility for things she can still handle. That would be the worst thing to do. I always encourage my elderly patients to push themselves as far as they can before transferring anything, to "shop 'til they drop." But I also warn them to make transference when they realize they simply can't cope with something, so as to protect their health and the quality of their lives.

The second thing to emphasize is that your elderly parent should be the decision-maker in the transference process. You should never try to force anyone to make a transference. If you know your mother or father is truly suffering from a dementing illness and can no longer handle any affairs, you have no choice. But if your parent is mentally alert but physically frail, you must work through that alert mind to get her to decide to let you assist her frail body.

While the elderly can make decisions, you must do everything in your power to help them make decisions that are healthy for them, decisions based on wisdom and not on fear. Take away their fear by gently urging them to decide which aspects of their lives have become tiresome and difficult, ones they would like not to have to do anymore. Then help them decide how, when, and to whom to transfer the responsibility.

Sometimes using a little humor or whimsy works well. For example, continuing the above scenario, you might whimsically relate your own need for a little help in your life: "Sometimes I wish a good fairy would just fly through this house and wave a magic wand and make it sparkle. Wouldn't that be great? Is there anything you'd like to have some help with? Maybe I could schedule the fairy two days a week."

Mom: "Is she good with numbers? My checkbook's a mess."
You: "I'm not sure about the fairy, but Bob's an accountant. How about letting him take a look at it?"

Bob may be your husband, or a brother, or even a neighbor. But he is somebody your mother knows and trusts. Your mother has now told you exactly where she needs help. And it may be the only thing with which she needs help. By assuming this one responsibility for her, you may be relieving enough of a load of worry that she is able to cope with everything else. Transferring only one or just a few responsibilities at first prevents your mother from thinking she's become a burden. It also sidesteps the issue of becoming dependent. When she makes the decision to let Bob help straighten out her checkbook, she maintains control over her life, her autonomy is not threatened, and her self-esteem is bolstered.

This is a simple illustration, but you should be getting the picture of how and why this technique works so well. It boils down to offering loving support in a nonthreatening way. It requires your understanding of the elderly person's feelings, a nonemotional approach, clear communication, and a huge dose of unconditional love.

Once you have reached a level of openness, communication and trust, it will be much easier for you and your parent to get involved in some very positive planning. Because your parent no longer fears losing control, she will be able to look to the future with much greater confidence. She knows she is an integral part of the planning, not just the object of it. She sees clearly now that she is still very much the active decision-maker in her life.

Prioritizing

The first step in your planning with your elderly parent should be prioritizing her needs. What is the single most important thing that is costing her quality in her life? Is it loneliness? Physical health? The inability to get places on her own? Financial pressure? Ask your parent to write a list of all the things she finds troublesome—everything, no matter how insignificant it may seem—if her feet hurt or if she is afraid of the neighbor's dog. The more you can get her to think about what is going on in her life, the more you will be able to draw her out to help you form a bigger, clearer picture on which to base your plans.

For example, if most of your mother's complaints are physical in nature, your first priority will be to attend to that aspect of her life. It is natural that aging parents are preoccupied with their physical health, for it is distressing to experience the effects of senescence. Helping to over-come this focus on failing physical health will release worry and make room for more positive thoughts and activities which will enhance life, things such as art, poetry, music, and friendships. I have already covered what is obvious when you need to address your parent's physical health—you, your parent and her primary care physicians must monitor her health with frequent evaluations, clean the slate concerning medications if necessary, and plan a wellness program for her.

Wellness is fast becoming the focus of our health care industry, because wellness is the only thing that will prevent a total overload of today's health care delivery system. With the numbers of elderly increasing each year, our society is obliged to not only try to change and evolve the cumbersome and ineffective system of health care delivery in our country but also to educate people on how to avoid the need for frequent medical treatment. Wellness is a holistic approach to physical health. It is more than just the avoidance of illness. It is a way to create and maintain homeostasis, or balance, in our lives. It incor-porates nutrition, physical exercise, stress management and self-care. I believe that every person, whatever age, needs to be aware of the benefits of designing and living with a wellness plan.

If such items as loneliness, isolation, and frustration at not being able to get around easily top your parent's list of things she'd like to change about her life, you can bet she is not getting enough mental and social stimulation. This is a major cause of the decline that leads to cir-cumstantial senility and is a serious problem among the elderly. When the energy to go and do things is limited, and the stress of having to arrange transportation and remember dates and times seems too much to cope with, many elderly people just give up and say, "To heck with it, it's not worth the effort." But it is worth the effort, for social and mental stimulation are all part of a general wellness approach to life.

Finances often crop up as a source of distress for the elderly. Sometimes it is something as simple as not being able to read the numbers in the checkbook and do the math correctly, but more often it is the feeling many elderly have that their savings and other resources are not enough. Without prying, you must learn about your parent's true financial state, for this will make a big difference in your planning.

Making Plans

Once you have the priorities clearly in mind, it is time to sit down in earnest with your elderly loved one and decide together how to address each. Sometimes by working on the single most important item, you can resolve some other problems automatically. For instance, if lack of energy is the primary problem, a change in dietary and exercise habits may not only result in increased energy, but also an increase in the person's ability to participate in social activities. Learning that your mother's hearing problem is preventing her from going to church, you can help her get a hearing aid, which not only remedies the immediate problem but also resolves several secondary concerns as well, including her loneliness and need for social stimulation and her need for spiritual involvement.

Understand that most elderly people are resistant to change, and keep your planning at a pace your parent can integrate, accept and cope with. Don't try to accomplish too much too soon. Take it one step at a time, one day at a time, and monitor the changes carefully as you go along.

Advanced Directives

One of the most important items on your planning agenda with your parent should be the development of a "living will" or "durable power of attorney." These two legal vehicles insure that your elderly parent's wishes will be respected, while at the same time protecting you and other family members—as well as health care professionals—should decisions need to be made on your parent's behalf if she should become unable to speak for herself.

Living Will. In 1974, as a result of the much-publicized Karen Anne Quinlan case, the concept of a "living will" was born. This is the most familiar of a type of legal instrument known as an "advanced directive," a document written and signed in advance of need, which makes clear a person's wishes about the use of life-prolonging medical procedures should she become terminally ill, or if death is imminent.

Although this was a giant step forward in protecting the legal and medical rights of terminally ill patients, the living will has been surrounded by controversy and confusion. All but nine states have enacted some sort of living will legislation, but in many cases, the statutes lack clarity and are written in vague language. In some cases, the statutes actually prevent the effective use of a living will as it was meant to be. There is much disparity between the laws of different states, and because of the federal government's position on states rights, there are many concerns as to whether a living will signed in one state will be upheld in another.

Durable Power of Attorney. Because of this, the American Bar Association created a new and broader vehicle, a version of the tried-and-true power of attorney called the "durable power of attorney" in which a proxy is appointed to speak for the incapacitated person. The proxy is able to discuss the patient's case with medical professionals and make decisions based on knowing what the patient would want rather than having a court-appointed guardian or other impersonal representative in control. This also relieves the family and physicians of making difficult decisions in times of stress.

This newer advanced directive is much broader in scope than the living will. It applies to the whole range of health care procedures, not just those regarding the prolonging of life by artificial means. It can actually work both ways, insuring a patient's desire for every possible life-saving measure to be used, if that is what is directed.

Whereas a general power of attorney is revoked if the maker becomes incompetent, the "durable" power of attorney remains in place until and unless the maker revokes it herself. The word "durable" must be used when writing such an instrument in order to protect the power of the proxy decision-maker named. The durable power of attorney can be used specifically for health care directives, or it can be much broader in scope, including financial and legal matters.

A recent survey showed that eighty to eighty-eight percent of the American public believed that individuals or their families should have control over decisions concerning their medical treatment or that of their next of kin, but only fifteen percent ever do anything to make sure their wishes are followed, primarily because they think it is too complicated or costly. Actually, executing a living will or durable power of attorney is quite simple. The forms are short, easy to read, and available free of charge. You do not need an attorney to complete an advanced directive; it can be as simple as writing a letter. For more complicated durable powers of attorney, however, I would recommend the use of a lawyer.

In discussing advanced directives with your parent, you must at all times be gentle and not imply that you think she is incompetent. The beauty of such a directive is that it is made by the elderly person, in advance, thereby keeping her in charge of her decision-making. You are wresting nothing from her; rather you are supporting her in maintaining control of her life to the very end. (See Appendix A for resources for more information about advanced directives.)

Before I move on I would like to share a story about a family whose foresight and intergenerational planning provided for a happy, secure, and nonproblematic old age for the elderly, widowed mother.

A former patient, Peggy, a widow in her late fifties, was diagnosed as having Parkinson's disease. She lived alone in the home she and her husband had purchased shortly after World War II. Proud and independent, this woman was determined to stay that way as long as she could, but she realized the limitations her disease would eventually impose on her. Her first action was to learn everything she could about her progressive disease. She discovered that probably she would live another fifteen or twenty years, but that as each year passed, she would lose some of her ability to get around on her own. She learned that unless she was taken by some other disease or accident, she would eventually suffer a form of true dementia and be totally unable to care for herself.

It was not easy for her to accept such a destiny, but she did, and then with clear, unemotional thinking, she and her adult children made plans together to organize her life and prepare for eventualities. Knowing she would be unable to meet the physical demands of managing a house on her own, she and her son, who was in real estate, painted her home and got it ready for sale. At the same time, Peggy and her children researched life care retirement facilities in the area and found one to her liking and that she could afford. When the house was sold, she invested part of the proceeds in an endowment program at the retirement center. It was a bright, pleasant facility where there were many activities, excellent meal service, and 24-hour emergency help should she need it. There she could retain her independence, living in her own apartment with her own personal belongings, until she physically was no longer able to manage by herself. Her investment insured that she would be cared for through the years as her disease progressed, even to the point of receiving intensive nursing care should she need it. She found great peace of mind in knowing that she had things handled and would never be a burden to her children.

The retirement center was in the same community where she had always lived, so she was able to stay involved in her former social activities. Several of her friends eventually moved into the complex as well. Because she was no longer tied down to caring for a house, she had more free time to enjoy other activities, and she joined a water exercise class to keep her muscles as strong as she could to counteract the effects of Parkinson's disease on the muscular system. She executed a living will to free her children of the decision of whether to continue the use of extraordinary life-sustaining measures should her condition deteriorate to the point where there was no quality of life left.

In short, this woman was in control of her life to the very end, because she planned with her family to transfer her affairs into the hands of others as it became necessary. The result was that her son and daughter-in-law, the only children living in the same town, were not "sandwiched"; her other two children who lived half a continent away knew she was happy and properly cared for; she retained her vital self-esteem; and many, many family problems were avoided.

6

Alternative
Living Arrangements

Peggy's story in the last chapter illustrates one of the many alternatives that are available today for your aging parents. There are many options, from receiving help while remaining in their home to relocating to an appropriate place, like Peggy did, where needs can be better met. As you plan together, consider all the possibilities and decide what makes the most sense, both for your aging parents and for yourself and your family.

In my two decades of serving the elderly in my community, it has become clear to me that as they age, older people need smaller, more service-rich environments. Being less able to integrate a lot of information mentally, the elderly cope by cutting down on the number of activities they undertake. Naturally, the basic activities of daily living take priority. Such things as meals, personal hygiene, and housekeeping, although important to their well-being, may begin to take all of their time, leaving the older person with no time, energy or mental capacity left over to participate in the "fun" aspects of life that add quality to their existence. For instance, when making decisions about what to eat and grocery purchases takes a person's full mental capacity and drains her energy reserves, spending an afternoon with friends becomes too much to cope with. Or when sorting and folding the laundry is all she can mentally cope with in a day, reading a book becomes out of the question.

Those of us still in our prime have difficulty conceiving that carrying out everyday activities such as these could so completely drain a person, both mentally and physically. The elderly experiencing the frustration of senescence understand the situation all too well. Many spend all their time, mental concentration, and physical energy simply maintaining a daily existence, and consequently their quality of life suffers tremendously. Moreover, the fear of losing the ability to manage for themselves leads to emotional decision-making, which only intensifies their anxieties and insecurity. They begin to lose the ability to cope, and finally their initial innocent act of withdrawal leads to isolation from life. We're back to our old nemesis, circumstantial senility.

If the demands made upon the elderly to accomplish their activities of daily living are reduced, however, they can maintain a much higher quality of life. In a smaller, service-rich environment, decisions about the activities of daily living—about meals, laundry, housework, shopping; even bathing, toileting, and personal grooming—can be handled by others, leaving the elderly with the energy and mental capacity to enjoy a movie, go to a concert, or take a walk. It is so beneficial it could almost be considered as part of a total wellness plan.

Many residential care facilities are providing such service-rich environments to their senior residents today, and at a far lower cost than nursing home care. By assuming the "life support" activities, many senior living facilities have freed their older residents to enjoy other, more mentally stimulating avocations. It was this type of facility that enabled Peggy to retain her autonomy, dignity and self-esteem. It also made it easier for her to cope with the disease she had contracted.

A Change in the Industry

With the growing number of elderly in our country, the entire health care delivery system has had to change, and in doing so, has wrought many changes in housing for the elderly. Once, the nursing home served not only as a place where patients received critical nursing care, but also as a warehouse for the elderly who had nowhere else to go. Many so-called patients were not sick. They were just old and frail and needed assistance with their ADLs.

Today, the skilled nursing facility is more what its name implies, a place where people of all ages go to recover from surgeries and extended illnesses, although many still house a large population of the elderly. The reason for this evolution is that because of the high cost of hospital care, hospitals are releasing patients quicker and sicker. They are not recovered sufficiently to return home, so they are released into a skilled nursing facility. These facilities are now in the business of rehabilitation, convalescence, and terminal care rather than housing for the elderly. Today, only 5 percent of those over 65 live in a skilled nursing center.

This push downward from the top of the health care system has led to the development of an entirely new industry in the last two decades: residential care facilities for the elderly. Because this is such a young industry, there is much confusion about what is available, what levels of care are offered, even what they are called. "Retirement residences" of all sizes and descriptions abound, ranging from the small residential care facilities mentioned above, to massive, planned communities such as Sun City. Basically, though, there are only three options, *Supportive Living*, *Catered Living*, and *Leisure Living*, all of which I describe later in this chapter.

LIVING ARRANGEMENTS CONTINUUM

Recognizing the value of the elderly maintaining their autonomy for as long as they can, while realizing that many need some sort of support to achieve that autonomy, I have created what I call a long term care *living arrangements continuum*. This is a plan under which the elderly can retain as much autonomy in their lives as they can handle while receiving assistance in those areas that absorb too much of their mental energies and take away from activities that provide a higher quality of life. Figure 6.1 illustrates this continuum and the three major categories of living arrangements that are available. Levels of service and supervision are at their lowest on the bottom of the continuum and increase as you move up. Levels of independence are at their highest on the bottom of the continuum model and decrease as the resident ages and becomes more frail.

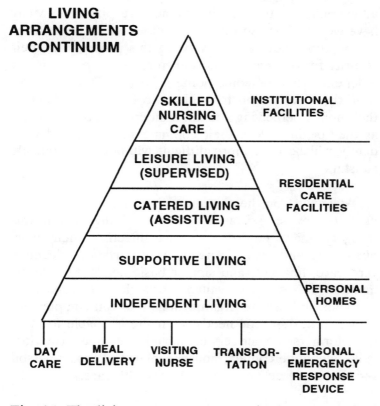

LIVING ARRANGEMENTS CONTINUUM

SKILLED NURSING CARE — INSTITUTIONAL FACILITIES

LEISURE LIVING (SUPERVISED)

CATERED LIVING (ASSISTIVE) — RESIDENTIAL CARE FACILITIES

SUPPORTIVE LIVING

INDEPENDENT LIVING — PERSONAL HOMES

DAY CARE | MEAL DELIVERY | VISITING NURSE | TRANSPORTATION | PERSONAL EMERGENCY RESPONSE DEVICE

Fig. 6.1. The living arrangements continuum.

Let us look at how the continuum can work to enhance the lives of the elderly.

Level 1. Personal Homes

Nearly all elderly people want to remain in their familiar home environments, to be able to age in place. Their attachments to their family homes are powerful. Many have worked hard so that their homes would be paid for by the time they retired, viewing this property as their security for old age. Perhaps even more important is the independence a personal home represents. As they grow frail, the elderly tend to hold on to the environment of their home, perceiving it to allow independence. However, as they begin to lose their coping skills, living independently will become more difficult without some outside assistance.

At Level 1 on the continuum, outside services can be used to provide assistance as needed. Individuals in this category may require assistance meeting their daily nutritional and hygienic needs, transportation, cleaning, yard care, finances, and similar basic needs. Most communities have services available through various charities, churches and private organizations that can complement your parent's specific needs when she is unable to meet them for herself. Such services include volunteer visitation, daily telephone contact, housekeeping and repair person services, meal delivery, and home health care.

If your parent needs help in one or more of these areas, contact your *Area Agency on Aging* (see Resources for Caregivers at the back of the book) to find out what is available and what such services cost. Many are free, while others, such as a visiting nurse or therapist who provides professional medical care, may cost as much as fifty dollars or more for one visit. These costs may or may not be allowable by *Medicare*, *Medicaid* and *Medigap* insurance. Consult with your parent's personal physician or social worker to find out what might be covered.

Case management. If you do not live near your aging parent, you may be able to find a qualified case manager who can monitor her care needs. A case manager assesses a person's total situation and then arranges to see that needed care is provided. Often, your Area Agency on Aging provides case management at no charge, or on a sliding scale. There are also private firms specializing in case management for a fee. The cost of case management is not covered by *Medicare*.

Socialization. If social isolation is one of your parent's problems, look into community services she could become involved in outside the home. In response to the growing need of families to provide care for elderly parents, *adult day care centers* and *senior activity centers* have sprung up across the country. Much as a children's day care center provides for the needs of the very young while parents work, adult day care centers provide for the needs of aging adults, including health care and social services, and one or two meals a day. Senior activity centers offer social activities and entertainment, but usually do not have a health care capability.

Whether your parent lives with you or not, adult day care centers or senior activity centers can meet her need to interact with others her age and to participate in activities that keep her mind and body active. Churches, hospitals, nursing homes, and private operators are all becoming involved in providing these services, and again, I suggest you contact your Area Agency on Aging for referrals.

Safety. Aging in place is important, and you should encourage your parents to remain in their family home as long as they can meet their ADLs. There are many ways you can ease this by helping your parent make her home safer. Accident prevention must be a serious consideration. Approximately 23,000 elderly Americans suffer *fatal* environmental accidents each year, more than half involving falling. Each year, over 150,000 elderly have a serious fall resulting in physical injuries ranging from severe bruising to hip fractures. The elderly fear falling almost as much as they fear senility.

Homes can be made safer by making changes that adapt to the dulling of the senses that comes with senescence. Lighting should be increased throughout the home. Brighter lights, more of them, and specialized lights, such as spotlights in areas where reading and work activities are enjoyed, can enhance both safety and convenience. Special attention should be paid to lighting in stairways, bathrooms and kitchens. Night-lights are a must. Light switches should be placed so lights and lamps can be turned on when entering a room, and the height of light switches and electrical outlets should be adjusted to compensate for disabilities.

Television sets should be easily accessible with room lighting adjusted so that it is neither too dim nor too bright. Two television sets may be a good idea if considerable time is spent in different parts of the house. Since the ability of the human eye to adjust for color perception decreases with age, images on black and white television sets often provide greater contrast and more comfortable viewing. Television controls should be understandable and easy to operate. Numbers should be large and clearly visible. Remote control devices may be helpful but numbers and channel selection devices should be easy to see and to use.

Appliances and telephones should be equipped with dials marked with large numbers. The OFF position should be marked clearly on all appliances. Loose fitting clothing is highly susceptible to catching fire and should not be worn in the kitchen or near other areas where fires are a hazard. If possible, open flame heaters should be replaced with devices less likely to cause fire. Emergency telephone numbers should be written in large print and kept near the telephone.

Floor surfaces should be painted or carpeted so there is a clear distinction between stair steps, floor surfaces and thresholds. Contrasting colors should be used when possible. Walkways should be clear of electrical cords, footstools and other low objects. Furniture should be kept in familiar locations providing landmarks for navigation.

Medication should be stored so that those taken internally are clearly distinguishable from those taken externally. Medicines should be positively marked and placed in consistent locations to avoid mistaken identities. Magnifying glasses stored in or near the medicine cabinet can be helpful in reading medication labels and other small print.

Hearing loss can become a safety hazard, too. Hearing aids should be used, and people talking to a hearing impaired elder should be sensitive to their impairment, making sure that the elderly person understands what is being said. Speak slowly and face the person directly. Use gestures and facial expressions to enhance communications. Be aware, though, that excessive gesturing can cause distractions for the listener. If the information is important, such as instructions for taking medication, write it down, then go over the instructions verbally. Leave a note in a conspicuous spot for future reference. Devices are available to enhance both hearing and speaking when using the telephone.

Diminished senses of taste and smell can be particularly dangerous for the elderly. Spoiled food may go undetected and may be inadvertently eaten. More seriously, the older person may fail to smell smoke or gas. Smoke detectors with direct connections to emergency fire and ambulance services could be life-saving.

Touch and balance control affect personal navigational ability. Carpets and rugs should be firmly attached to the floor. Rugs at the top of stairs should be removed. Uneven floor surfaces should be eliminated or clearly marked when elimination is not possible. Nonslip wax or carpeting should be on all floor surfaces. Handrailings should be installed on all stairways both inside and outside the home. Railings should be installed on tubs and near toilets and nonslip pads should be installed in showers and tubs. Favorite chairs should provide firm support and have solid arms that are useful in rising from the seated position. Pedestal tables should be anchored securely to the floor. Shelves should be arranged so no climbing or extreme stretching is necessary. Frequently used objects should be placed in easy reach.

Many of these suggestions may seem like common sense for any household, yet, from the high incidence of accidents among the elderly, clearly not enough homes have been enhanced for safety. If your parents are mentally and physically able to age in place in their own home, help them do so by personally assessing their living environment for safety hazards and make changes as necessary.

Special Assistive Equipment. Some elderly individuals are perfectly able to function on their own except for vision or hearing impairments or the inability to move about freely. You may be able to procure specialized equipment that will enable your parent to compensate for such losses and by that allow her to age in place in her own home longer.

A variety of products is available for the vision impaired, including watches with braille or very large type, telephone attachments with large numbers on the dial pad, kitchen utensils with large markings, medical equipment, large-type and tape-recorded books, and newspaper reading services. The address for *The Lighthouse for the Blind* is included in the appendix, Resources for Caregivers.

For those suffering a hearing loss, besides hearing aids, there are devices that alert the individual when the phone, doorbell or alarm clock rings or the smoke detector goes off. Adapters are available for telephones that amplify the caller's voice. Some television is now broadcast with captions for the hearing impaired, and there are also adapters for television sets that provide captions for regular programming.

Walkers, wheel chairs, and canes have traditionally provided greater mobility for the elderly, if the person will use them properly and not feel it is undignified. Such devices help tremendously in preventing the falls I mentioned earlier, and you should encourage your elderly parent to use some sort of supportive devices as these if her mobility is impaired. Another excellent idea is to install grab bars in areas of her home where she is most likely to walk, such as hallways, bathrooms and kitchens.

In cases where a frail elderly parent lives alone, you may wish to purchase a personal emergency response device that can be used to summon help from a central response center such as a hospital in the area. The initial purchase price for such a device may be as much as five hundred dollars, and you will pay a monthly fee to the response center also. Some devices are available for lease, and in some areas may be provided free for financially qualified persons. Not all elderly people need such systems, but it may give both you and your parent greater peace of mind about her remaining in her own home.

Level 2. Residential Care Facilities

If you and your parent find it is not in her best interest to age in place, if her health is failing or her frailty is too extreme, you must take great care in evaluating the alternatives. You are making an environmental decision that will affect the quality, and sometimes, even the length of her life. Her new surroundings will, in essence, replace the family environment, and it is critical to make sure the new home setting is appropriate.

Supportive Living. Your first decision will be whether your parent can live happily and safely in a residential setting or if she needs skilled nursing care. If you feel she can live fairly autonomously, needing only moderate assistance in living, you should get your parent to consider moving up one step on the continuum into a supportive living arrangement in a residential care facility.

In talking about a residential care facility, I want to make it clear that I do not mean a nursing home! This type of facility is a residential setting offering needed support services on a noninvasive basis while allowing residents to maintain autonomy and personal independence. There are three levels of care within the scope of residential care facility, *Supportive, Catered*, and *Leisure Living*. In most states these facilities are licensed as *Adult Congregate Living Facilities* (ACLFs).

Residential care facilities can be large or small. The smaller ones used to be called "board and care" homes. In a small residential care facility, a person pays rent and receives—besides a room—meals, housekeeping, utilities, laundry, and monitoring by a paid staff member. Usually these homes are located in neighborhoods and run by private families, although many, such as my *Just Like Home* (R) facilities, are evolving and offering professional, more sophisticated programs. At *Just Like Home* residences, care is designed along a social model, with trained companion caregivers providing assistance with ADLs to those who live there. We include structured activities and transportation so residents receive the social stimulation they need and can maintain their independence to a high degree.

If you and your parent opt for a small residential care facility, be sure to check it out thoroughly. If it is licensed, find out if any deficiencies have been noted in the recent past. Be sure what services your parent will be receiving. Currently, the cost for these facilities runs between $950 and $2,300 per month.

Supportive Living programs also are often offered in a 100 to 200-unit apartment-type complex that provides one communal meal a day, linen, laundry and housecleaning services, transportation, environmental security, coordination of health care, and planned recreational activities.

For many elderly, a Supportive Living Facility provides more than just services that allow them to cope with the intrinsic problems of aging; these types of communities also become the source for valuable social interaction and mental stimulation as well. For some individuals, just relocating to such a place can reverse the deterioration that leads to circumstantial senility.

Catered Living. As residents continue to age in place in a Supportive Living Facility, they may begin to require more services than can be provided in this environment. Rather than one prepared meal a day, they may require three. Rather than just linen laundry services, they may require personal laundry service as well. They may require supervision to insure their medication is taken correctly. At this stage, when physical frailty increases and the resident needs more assisted care, it makes sense for them to advance to a Catered Living level. Fortunately, many newer retirement centers offer more than one level of care, which allows residents to remain in the same social network while moving into the next level of care.

Catered Living facilities are often homes in residential areas with fifty to sixty units per home, much like a fraternity or sorority house. They provide smaller amounts of personal space, a private or shared bedroom and bath, with common spaces for all residents to enjoy. The common spaces inhibit withdrawal and encourage group associations. Noninvasive supervisory intervention is much easier in this environment. Costs range from $1,350 to $3,500 per month.

Leisure Living. Residents whose cognitive (thinking) abilities are seriously impaired may require even more supervision and the intensified services of a Leisure Living Facility. This is a new approach to the care of those residents suffering from the true dementias such as Alzheimer's and multi-infarct dementia. Instead of relegating them to an institutional setting where they may undergo the degradation of being physically restrained or sedated, a Leisure Living setting provides a quiet, reality-oriented environment where these people can still maintain much of their personal freedom. In such a place, the staff is specially trained to meet the needs of the demented elderly, including the recognition that too much stimulation creates stress for them. The caregivers in this type of facility help residents keep things simple in their lives, protect them from becoming emotionally overloaded by their surroundings, and help them "find their quiet" when they become frustrated or overstressed. Residents almost invariably develop a high level of trust in their caregivers and establish a transference relationship with the staff.

Such residences will generally have no more than sixteen units and offer a full range of basic and extended care services. Because, for the most part, the residents in a Leisure Living facility do not require skilled nursing, the staff administers minimal medical care. You could expect to pay from $1,600 to $4,000 per month for a Leisure Living type of facility.

Level 3. Institutional

For those whose physical needs become too complex to allow them to remain in these more independent types of environments, living in an Institutional Facility may be unavoidable. When a person needs intensive nursing care, a skilled nursing facility (SNF) or convalescent hospital is appropriate. Unfortunately, when a person is placed in this setting, her autonomy is often collapsed, and it is important to try to avoid this level until all others have been explored. Today, care in a skilled nursing facility costs between $2,400 and $6,000 per month.

Continuing Care Retirement Communities

One type of senior living arrangement that has evolved over the past several decades is the "life care" facility, which incorporates all three assisted living levels plus skilled nursing. A life care or *Continuing Care Retirement Community* (CCRC), differs from small residential "board and care" homes and most other types of ACLFs in that for an initial entry fee, as well as monthly maintenance and service fees, a person will receive care for life, no matter what their physical or mental capabilities may become. A life care residence usually offers Supportive

Living, Catered Living, Leisure Living and Skilled Nursing Care all under one roof, or at least on the same campus.

The cost of entering a life care community can range from $25,000 to $500,000, depending upon location, quality, and the range of services offered. Monthly services fees range from $800 to $3,500 per month. At first, these were mostly annuity-based. This meant that a person gave up all assets in return for being taken care of for life. This evolved into paying a specific fee, plus buying monthly services at a fixed rate. Later, the monthly fees began to fluctuate depending upon costs. Today, many life care facilities require an entry fee, part of which is refundable, plus a fluctuating monthly rate and fees for specific services. The trend seems to be very much toward a fee-for-service basis.

Some CCRCs have experienced financial difficulties, because their projections were based upon their residents having a shorter life expectancy than has become the reality today. In other words, the turnover has not been as frequent as expected, and as a result, the income has not reached levels great enough to sustain operations. If you and your parent want to consider this type of facility, be sure you and your attorney examine its financial statement, specifically noting the cash reserves and how they are used. Check with the *Better Business Bureau* or *Consumer Protection Agency* in the area to be sure no complaints have been made against the residence. Although life care facilities offer many advantages, including being able to remain in one place as a person's need for services move up the continuum, it should be "buyer be very informed" when investigating this option.

Making the Choice

When you and your parent are certain that a move is required, visit several residential care and/or nursing facilities (depending on the level of care your parent needs). Take the tour offered by the marketing people, but also make time to talk about the program offered at each place. Too often people look at the cosmetics of a facility, rather than the services and philosophy behind the operation. Some facilities, both residential and skilled nursing, are appealing to the eye, but the program of care and services offered invades a person's privacy or diminishes her autonomy, both of which can lead to depression and circumstantial senility.

To help you evaluate which facility would best meet your parent's needs, list the following items and answer these and any other questions you think of. Write as complete a description of each as you and your parent can remember after your tour. Use a separate sheet for each facility you visit.

1. Costs: Is there an up-front entry fee? If so, is it refundable? What is the rent amount? What services are included? What is available at additional cost?

2. Physical plant: How well are the buildings and grounds kept up? (Look at the ceilings for telltale signs of roof leaks.) Are the rooms or apartments freshly painted? Is the carpeting clean and in good repair? What is the air quality? Is the decor appealing? Are there common areas for social activities? What size are the apartments? Can a person bring her own furnishings?

3. How residents act: Do they appear neat and clean? Happy? Are nursing patients unrestrained? Are there structured activities? What kind?

4. Meal service: Is the food tasty, nourishing, and eye-appealing? What meals are served? Is there a kitchen in the apartments? Can the facility adapt to special dietary needs?

5. Health care: Is there 24-hour staff on the premises? Are medications supervised? What level of nursing qualifications do those on the nursing staff hold? What other health-related services are offered, i.e. physical therapy, podiatrist, exercise room, swimming pool, and so forth.

6. Transportation: Is transportation provided? In what type of vehicle? Is it equipped with easy access for the handicapped? Is the cost included in rent/service fees? How often is it available, and how wide a range does it cover?

7. Scope of services: What levels of care are offered? Will your parent be able to age in place as her needs become greater?

8. Attitude of the management: Are your questions answered promptly and courteously? Is the staff appropriately dressed and well-groomed?

9. Financial stability: Who owns the facility and what are that person's/corporation's qualifications for operating such a residence? What is its credit rating with suppliers?

What cash reserves are on hand, and what is the policy for expending these?

10. Overall ambience: Did you get a good feeling while you were in the facility? Did you notice anything unpleasant?

Perhaps the most important question to answer in advance is: How does the facility and its staff encourage residents to retain their autonomy and independence? I promote the idea of a service-rich environment in elderly housing, but not to the point where residents no longer have any motivation to meet as many of their ADLs and IADLs as they can manage. If the program in a facility either (1) invades a person's privacy or (2) diminishes her autonomy, stay away.

Financial Considerations

The cost of long-term care, whether at home, in a residential care facility, or in a skilled nursing facility, all too often is not covered by Medicare and rarely by other forms of acute care medical insurance. Medicaid, a government-funded medical assistance program, helps only those living at or below the poverty level. Affordable private insurance is becoming more available to cover the cost of long term care. However, this is a relatively new insurance product, with many variables and price tags. Shop the market before purchasing such a policy, and make sure you compare "apples to apples" when evaluating benefits and premiums.

Unfortunately, there has been exploitation of the elderly by unscrupulous people in the residential care, insurance, and health care supply and service industries and many elderly and their families are skeptical, fearing such exploitation. Your best defense against exploitation and manipulation is to seek the answers you need from bona fide services for the elderly. (See Resources for Caregivers for a list of reference sources you can trust.) Educate yourself and your parent before making any decisions, and if possible, make all decisions ahead of the need.

Other Options

Granny Flats. "Granny flats" are an option for some families. A granny flat is a separate apartment on the same property as the main household that allows the elderly person to retain a certain amount of autonomy and independence while having younger family members nearby in case she needs assistance. Granny flats can be converted garages, home additions, separate houses, and in some areas, even mobile homes. Zoning and neighborhood association restrictions must be investigated and considered before making a decision to use this alternative.

Shared Housing. Sometimes the best solution is for an elderly person to share her family home with another person or persons. This is not taking in boarders per se. It is more like having roommates. The advantage to this arrangement is that it provides an informal support system for your parent without cost. Great caution should be taken, however, in selecting a person or persons to share your parent's home. There are many freeloaders and con artists who prey on the vulnerable elderly. I have already discussed the dangers of caregiver prejudice, and it is just as likely your parent could make inappropriate counter-transference to a roommate as to a caregiver.

Any shared housing arrangement should be put in writing. For example, if the roommate is to pay rent, a rental agreement should be signed. If the roommate is to provide some services, such as housekeeping, cooking, shopping, or yard work in exchange for lodging, this, too should be put in writing so there are no misunderstand-ings. Open communications between those who share a household is critical. Whether your parent shares her house or moves into another's home, all rights and respon-sibilities should be carefully delineated ahead of time.

Moving in with Children. There are instances when moving an elderly parent into your home is the only viable option that finances will allow or that either generation wants. Understand, however, that this generation of elderly wants intimacy at a distance, and take care to try to arrange your home so that your elderly parent can have a room to herself if possible. Privacy is important, both for your family and for your elderly loved one. Having a place to get away from each other can smooth the rough edges when one generation steps on another's feelings, which is going to happen from time to time.

Try to integrate Mom or Dad into your household routine. If they are physically able, assign some meaningful household chores. This will relieve you of some drudge work and make your parent feel more at home. Take advantage of your parent's skills. If your dad is handy with a hammer and screwdriver, let him become the household handyman. If your mother likes to cook, let her. You do not have to take all the extra responsibility onto your shoulders alone. Let your kids pitch in, too. If they are teenagers, they're old enough to learn to do the laundry, including the ironing. They may grumble about this some, but if everyone approaches the situation with understanding and good humor, integrating another generation into the household may be a particularly rewarding experience.

One very positive aspect of having a grandparent around the house is that it offers an excellent opportunity for the older person to share her wisdom and heritage. Without encouraging commiseration about the good old days, urge your parent to tell stories about what happened in her youth. It is living history, and if you venerate your parent and let her know how meaningful and enjoyable it is to you and your family to hear what life was like three quarters of a century ago, you will all come away with a new respect for one another.

Ideally, the decision to change the living environment of an elderly person is made to maintain the quality of her life, but the quality and sanctity of the lives of the family members who serve as caregivers must be considered equally valuable. The stress of caring for your aging parent can erode the quality of your life and that of your own family, and this reality must be considered when making decisions with your parent concerning her living arrangements. In the next chapter, I will discuss further some coping techniques you might need to call upon if your parent does move into your household. But before you and your parent make any decisions, you should first carefully evaluate her situation to see just which level of care she needs.

Evaluating Abilities for Independent Living

Moving is disruptive at any stage of life, but it is especially difficult for those who are older. Therefore, before making any decisions to move your elderly parent anywhere, you must first evaluate her abilities carefully to decide what level of care would be most beneficial. The three key areas that should be evaluated are: (1) basic activities of daily living, (2) instrumental activities of daily living, and (3) cognitive strengths.

Basic Activities of Daily Living. These activities include bathing, dressing, toileting, independent mobility, eating and grooming. Can your parent do these things without help? Is some help required from a spouse or other family members? Is your parent unable to take care of these needs independently at all?

Instrumental Activities of Daily Living. These include tasks that require higher skills, such as the ability to walk to and from places within walking distance, do grocery and clothes shopping, prepare meals, and other than investments, control and manage money. To what degree can your parent accomplish these activities independently, if at all?

Cognitive Strengths. This includes orientation to people, place and time, recent and remote memory, and behavior patterns. Is your parent noticeably confused or disoriented? Does she have difficulty remembering? Has your parent recently displayed any unusual changes in behavior? Has there been any particularly stressful life events, such as the death of a loved one, sickness, or financial hardship?

Beyond evaluating these three key points, other factors should be evaluated as well, including the person's general physical condition, musculoskeletal impairments, physical strength and other specific health risks.

Avoid Crisis Decision-making

Decisions made in times of crisis are not usually as well thought out as they should be, and mistakes may be hard to rectify. Statistics show that forty percent of all placements of the elderly in nursing homes occurs without prior discussion with the person involved. Instead of carefully planning for possible eventualities with the elderly, their children often make a decision to relocate a loved one when there is an unexpected crisis. Understandably, this produces a great deal of anxiety for the person being relocated and guilt for the family making the decision. It may have a devastating effect on relationships, one that will take a long time to overcome. Sometimes, it can become so disruptive that normal relationships between the elderly and their loved ones who initiate the move are never reestablished.

Crisis decision-making can also result in placement in the wrong environment and can be worse than if the elderly were allowed to stay put. If your parent is moved into an environment that decreases her autonomy any more than is necessary, she may react by becoming even more passive and withdrawn, defeating the whole purpose of the move. Or if she is thrust into a situation where she can no longer experience intimacy at a distance, where her life become disordered and she has little privacy or time alone, she may react with belligerence and abusive behavior. And when you think about it, who can blame her? In both cases, she has lost control.

Crisis decision-making in determining an appropriate living environment for the elderly usually represents invasive intervention. Sometimes, of course, it cannot be avoided. But more often than you might think, the decision to relocate your elderly parent can be accomplished in a more positive manner and with better results through noninvasive intervention and including the elderly in the decision-making process.

Whose Decision Is It?

As eager as you may be to help decide what living arrangement is best for your parent, you must realize that all evaluations and resulting decisions must be made with her, not for her. She should always be involved in the decisions being made about her life, provided of course that she is mentally able to participate. These evaluations need not be stressful nor must they invoke feelings of insecurity. As long as communications are open and both parties feel confident that the evaluations are being performed jointly, objectively, and with your parent's best interests in mind, she will likely be receptive and accepting of the outcome.

Often when the elderly and their families work together to evaluate and make decisions about the care of the older generations, communications are opened and transference relationships are facilitated. Children may be surprised to find how much thought their parents have given to the subject and that alternatives have already been considered. This can be a time of family closeness, not stress. The key is making the evaluations and decisions in advance, if possible, and in a well-planned and noninvasive way.

7

A Caregiver's Survival Kit

"**I** feel so guilty all the time! I feel guilty that I'm not spending the time I should with my children; I feel guilty that I'm too tired to be a good lover to my husband. I love my mother, and I'm trying to do what's best for her, but I get so angry with her sometimes, and then I feel even more guilty!"

Marge's pent-up frustration spilled over with her tears that day in my office, and the only thing I had to offer her, besides a tissue, was one piece of advice: "Don't be so hard on yourself."

Don't feel guilty. Give yourself credit for all you are doing. You are being the best parent you can be to your children. You are being the best wife to your husband. There is a limit to everyone's energy, and if you have reached yours, recognize it. Pat yourself on the back, take hold of your guilt, and drop it. Give your attention to some ways you can ease the situation and get rid of the guilt feeling permanently.

Find Time For Yourself

To be an effective caregiver, you must first take care of yourself. To preserve your own mental health and quality of life, you must find time for yourself. You need to remove yourself at stated intervals from the tensions and stress involved in caregiving. Such a change of pace should help you overcome those negative feelings that build up and cause you to burn out. This is called *respite*.

Before you reach the breaking point, ask for help. Your brothers and sisters, or others in your immediate family should be willing to take over caregiving responsibilities for brief periods at frequent intervals to relieve you. But send out your SOS in a mature way. Plan your approach carefully. Avoid doing it at a time when you are feeling negative and stressed out. A negative approach, such as: "I'm sick of being the only one who ever looks out for Mom. It's your turn now" would put them on the defensive. It might be another's turn, but it would be better to use the old adage "honey catches more flies than vinegar." Were you to alienate them, they might well say: "Tough. You said you'd do it, so quit whining." If you do your best to establish healthy rapport with your siblings and others in your family, you will earn their gratitude. This is just as important as being able to communicate properly with your elderly parents.

Senior Day Care. If your family cannot help, you may be able to use a *senior day care center*, if there is one nearby. Such centers are equipped and staffed to care for the frail elderly for periods during the daytime hours. They are similar to day care centers for children. They usually offer activities, a social environment, and a nourishing mid-day meal. The cost is reasonable, and the benefits to you as an overburdened caregiver, are enormous.

Your first hurdle is to get your parent to try this option. The very idea may be so new you may need to use your most convincing arguments to make it seem an adventure worth her while. If all else fails, you may have to make the decision yourself. In order for you to continue as their caregiver, you simply must have some free time. Work patiently with her. Offer to be responsible for the outcome, and express your gratitude that she is prepared to cooperate so there will not be so much pressure on you. You may hesitate to make this decision, but seeking such respite may be for the benefit of both you and your parent long term.

Before enrolling your parent in any day care program, take time to visit the facility yourself and check out its program and personnel. Satisfy yourself that your parent will be well cared for. Keep in mind that although she may be reluctant to go at first, once she is there, she will find social stimulation, interesting activities and new friends within a very short time, and from then on, she will look forward to her days out.

Companions. It may be that your best alternative is to hire a companion to come into your home to care for your parent. Take great care in selecting such a companion. Some hired companions are wonderful, caring people. Others are in the business to prey on the vulnerability of the elderly. In more than one instance, elderly people have been induced to transfer money and other valuables to a hired caregiver who took advantage of the situation. So the applicant should be carefully checked out. Former employers should be contacted. References should be examined carefully. You, as a caregiver, will not experience relief from a stressful situation unless you have complete confidence in the companion.

In considering these options, it would be well to consult the aging network in your county or city. Your *Area Agency on Aging* should give you a list of day care programs and should also have the names of companions they can recommend. They may offer other suggestions that would prove most helpful and ease the situation considerably.

Dealing With Stress

Having to make such decisions is very stressful. We live in a stressful world, for stress is prevalent where there are negative physical and behavioral problems. You may be subject to stress and excuse yourself by saying, "I was so stressed out I got a migraine headache," or "The stress at work was so great that when I got home, I yelled at my wife and kids." This may ease the situation for the moment, but this is not an effective way to deal with stress.

Your emotional outburst will not remove the cause of stress. You must still deal with it. Eventually you will learn that your happiness does not depend on what is going on around you, but rather how you deal internally with these forces and events. Stress builds up when you respond to outer circumstances. You eliminate much of the stress when you take charge and, out of inner strength, control the situation.

For example, consider the mother bird who built her nest in a little tree next to a great waterfall. She sat on her nest of eggs in complete composure while only a few feet away, the mighty stream tumbled down on the rocks with such force, it sounded like thunder. Fine mist floated around the nest, but the bird calmly sat on the nest, waiting for the eggs to hatch. The bird was in control.

Inner control enables you to handle stressful situations. If your mother comes to live with you (an external event), and caring for her begins to cause you to feel anxiety and guilt (your internal reactions), you must find ways to get in control of the situation. Face what is wrong. What needs to be done to make her demands on your time and energy acceptable? When you take control, you may not change the outer circumstances, but you get rid of the stressful part of it.

This may seem easier said than done. You may say: "When I took control, I only got myself into more trouble. I thought I was facing up to the problem that Mom could not live alone any more when I decided she should come and live with us. But now I feel stress and fatigue and overwork because of my caregiving responsibilities."

You were capable of taking control of the situation when you brought your mother into your home. Now show the same control of this developing situation by make a decision about respite.

Protect Your Physical Health

Getting respite is only one necessary step you must take to care for yourself. As a caregiver, you must give serious attention to your physical health. Wellness is as important for you as it is for your elderly parent. Eat right. Get sufficient rest, including periods in the daytime, if your sleep is interrupted at night. Exercise regularly. These are the things the doctor and the media say are good—and they are right!

Pay attention to your body. If you begin having colds or infections, your body is saying, "Hey, you're neglecting me!" If you are listless or without energy, your body may be signaling you to get out for a walk in the fresh air and sunshine every day. And if you are less in control and are becoming increasingly dependent on tranquilizers, alcohol, or cigarettes to cope, your body, as well as your mind, is sending up a red flag for you to do appropriate problem-solving and decision-making to change what is going on in your life.

What About Your Social Health?

Your social health also is important. You may at first be overwhelmed by new demands on your time, but for your own good, continue as many of your social activities and contacts as is possible. You may be willing to sacrifice these to protect your loved one, but this can be hazardous to your health, and you may build up resentments. You may have to adjust your caregiving responsibilities, but it is imperative that you get on with your own life. Stay involved in activities and avocations that you enjoy. Do not allow your love life and your closeness with your mate to suffer. Have as your goal to keep your own life as balanced and normal as it was before you took on caregiving responsibilities. Use the suggestions I outlined above to restore a healthy mental outlook on life.

Saying Goodbye

You will be under a different form of stress immediately before and after your loved one passes away. If your parent is suffering an extended period of infirmity before dying, such as those who are victims of cancer and other degenerative diseases, she may need the help you can give or make available to prepare for the end. If you succeed in helping your loved one find fulfillment during her convalescence, she will be more relaxed and face the future less afraid. Helping your parent prepare for the changes that occur with death is perhaps the ultimate in the care you can render then. You may need to turn to a rabbi, priest or minister, if previous contacts have been made, to help you in this delicate matter.

Before you can be of much help to your parent at this time, you need to clarify your own ideas about death and deal with it positively. Help yourself, and your parent, overcome fear of death by acknowledging that death is a part of the cycle of life and will inevitably come to every one of us. As Shakespeare's Julius Caesar said: "Of all the wonders that I yet have heard, it seems to me most strange that men should fear, seeing that death, a necessary end, will come when it will come."

Rethink your idea of death. Instead of focusing on it as a loss, acknowledge that although death takes away a physical presence, it does not take away the importance of that person in your life, the influence she has had on you, or the love you have shared. These things will abide in your memory as long as you live. Celebrate them in honor of your parent. Recount them while your loved one is still alive, so she can be honored and uplifted by their memory as well. Such moments may be among the richest in both your lives.

As a physician, I have witnessed many deaths, and the vast majority occurred very peacefully. Usually, death was a spiritually meaningful event, not accompanied by pain, fear, anxiety or any threatening feelings. So death need not be fearful for either the dying or you as the caregiver.

Persons who have built an inner support system through their spiritual perspective on life tend to have less fear of death than those who are not spiritually motivated. Whether their system of thought includes a clear perception of life after death or not, people of faith are better able to deal with death than others. Whatever your religion, helping your parent define her own spiritual perspective, and examining your own as well, is one way to help you both get ready for the change that is inevitable.

The final days of life are made easier if you have helped your parent arrange financial matters to her satisfaction. See that your parent's will is updated. If she has no will, help her work with an attorney to write one so that her intentions will be honored and other members of the family will be satisfied that what has been written is your parent's and not your expressed wish.

See that your parent's estate is properly managed. It may be your parent's wish to divide the estate or household goods or heirlooms among family members while she is still able to act responsibly. You should encourage your parent to make independent decisions on these matters for as long as possible.

Another way to make the moment of death easier for all concerned is for the family, under your direction as the caregiver, to prearrange the funeral. Rather than act under the pressure, emotional tension and sadness at the time of death, decisions about funeral expenses, announcements, and those who will participate in the actual services may be made well in advance. Your parent may find added comfort in helping to draw up the ritual that is to be used at the time the family will say a final farewell.

Nor should the funeral be the only opportunity to say farewell. Nixon Waterman wrote: "A rose to the living is more, if graciously given before the hungering spirit is fled—a rose to the living is more than sumptuous wreaths to the dead." Close friends and relatives need not wait until the time of death to talk freely and intimately with the loved one. Letters, phone calls, visits, gatherings of family and friends with your parent will enable many to give thanks for the love and attention shown during a lifetime. How much better to affirm the words of gratitude while there is still life than to offer them after your loved one has departed. Make it a time of celebration, a time to heal old wounds among family members, a time to draw members of the family closer together. When this is not done, and death comes suddenly and unannounced, those who have not spoken may feel as if they have been robbed of the opportunity to say goodbye.

One final step in planning for death is recognizing the importance that ritual plays in helping you and your other family members adjust to life without your parent. Rituals are an important part of our lives. Weddings, communions, mitzvahs, and funerals all acknowledge the changes that come through the years. Although such rituals vary according to one's religious belief, they all stress the sanctity of life and the importance of love and tenderness in our human relationships. A funeral enables survivors to lend emotional support to one another, which helps tremendously in alleviating grief. You, your siblings, your children, and other family members and close friends can help one another move forward in your own lives by facing the pain and expressing your feelings openly when gathered after a death. Talking about the deceased person often brings up happy memories and funny incidents that help assuage the pain and guilt you feel over your loss.

The Cleansing Power of Grief

Grief flows naturally at the time of loss. Grief is nature's way of cleansing your emotions, allowing you to release your physical ties to the person who has died, and enabling you to get on with your life. Grief reactions usually move through a series of emotions. At first, there is disbelief: "A moment ago she was alive. Can it really be that she is gone now?" Then comes shock and possibly guilt. As the reality of the event takes hold of you, you are stunned and somewhat paralyzed, not knowing what you should do immediately, and then you reflect: "What could I have done that I didn't do?" Unless you are careful, you will have an overpowering sense of guilt.

As moments pass and you are more reflective, you may begin to accept what has happened, and at such a moment, you may even experience relief——relief that the tensions of caregiving are over, but even more, relief that the loved one is no longer in bondage to a condition that could not improve. At last, your loved one's spirit is free. You may also feel gratified, too, that you and your loved one took the time to anticipate this moment as you carry out the plans the two of you so carefully made.

The Three R's

A mature and thoughtful way to control your emotions following the death of your loved one could be called the "three Rs." This may prove an intellectual approach and help you handle the stress of decision-making at such a time.

The first R stands for *release*. You release your loved one physically, but you hold sacred her memory. Do not allow thoughts of your loss to be the center of your attention. The second R stands for *refocus*. Attempt to refocus your thinking on your need to get on with your life, realizing that you must live your days without your loved one. Your need to adjust to the new situation can be helped as you employ the third R——*regroup*. Regroup your thoughts. You may be helped as you think of the sanctity of life, both the life of your loved one and your own life. Live one day at a time. Instead of dwelling on your loss, encourage yourself to live each day in the joy of the present moment and what the future may bring. This will enable you to move forward with your life in a positive and productive way.

Using the three R's to help you past your grief does not take away the pain of your loss, but it can lessen it and bring you back to balance more quickly. If you have followed the above recommendations and prepared for the death of your loved one, such an approach to grief will prove to be natural. Those who have not, for one reason or another, prepared for the inevitable or who are unable to release the guilt they feel as a caregiver for the loss of a loved one, suffer an unnecessarily lengthy grieving period.

Death is the natural conclusion to life. Planning for death and having a positive approach to it can help you protect your loved one's human dignity to the very end of life and give her a feeling of control over her final stage of life. Then without fear, you will both find inner peace. Without stress, you can say goodbye.

8

A New Look
at Growing Old

A caregiver in a retirement community my company manages said to me, "I hope we get all the bugs worked out of the health care delivery system for the elderly before I get old." She was a farsighted young woman. Perhaps because she worked with the elderly daily, she recognized and verbalized exactly what must take place if we wish to avoid a national debacle when the baby boom generation reaches its seventies and eighties. That time is not far away . . . by the year 2016, the leading edge of the fifty-four million baby boomers will celebrate their seventieth birthdays, and chances are, if you are reading this book, you will be among them.

What about it? Have you thought much about your old age? Or have you been too preoccupied with care-giving to your children and elderly parents to be concerned about your future? If you have been caught in the Sandwich Generation, the time to prevent that happening to your children is now. In the previous chapters, I have emphasized the importance of planning, and it is time for everyone over the age of forty to begin to look ahead and plan, with their children, for their later years.

A New Generation of Elderly

As I said earlier, the elderly of today have been a coping generation, facing many struggles just to survive. There's no doubt they are living older longer. Unlike them, the elderly of tomorrow—those who are in their middle years now—have had the privilege to focus more on living well, rather than just coping with life, and as you age, you will enjoy living younger longer. Your generation has had many advantages never dreamed of by former generations. Inoculations when you were babies prevented such childhood scourges as measles, mumps, scarlet fever, polio, and other diseases that cost many in earlier generations their good health, sometimes even their lives. You have had the benefits of better education, with many more in our population achieving college degrees than ever before. The tremendous scientific and technological advances, which have resulted from the space program and other research, have introduced miracles such as organ transplants, lap top computers, and air bags in automobiles. Because so many of you in today's middle generation have a better education, many also have been able to achieve greater financial security than your parents could.

In short, as a generation you are healthier, better educated, and financially more secure than any generation that has come before. It follows logically that you will also be different in some ways than the elderly of today when you reach old age, and that you will demand more from life, the health care system, your government, and perhaps even yourselves. Health and fitness equipment will likely be installed in your retirement condo right along with the security handrails. You will probably demand sprouts on your tofuburgers in the dining room. And the laundry will find ways to make sure your Nike sneakers come out white after you've scuffed them on the walking path.

Yes, as a generation, you have many advantages as you enter your later years, but that does not mean you won't have to deal with the effects of senescence. We will all grow old, and your generation will probably grow older than any that have gone before. Already, many elderly are celebrating their ninetieth or even hundredth birthdays. Are you ready to deal with living to one hundred and ten? If you are only forty now, or fifty, or sixty, think of the many years you still have, and how you can prepare to make them the best years of your life.

A Strategic Plan for Growing Old

Just as many businesses develop a strategic plan to help them grow and prosper, you can develop a strategic plan for successful living in your later years. There are four areas you should concern yourself with in creating such a plan: (1) retirement and productivity, (2) finances, (3) health, and (4) family relations.

In spite of the generally accepted theory that retirement should be something of a perpetual vacation, the need for an ordered, goal-oriented life does not stop when you retire from your career. I have shown that feeling nonproductive is a main cause of decline among the elderly. When you are still in the swing of things at work, at home, and at play, it's hard to consider what it would be like any other way. But when you reach that magic age of sixty-five, or whenever you opt to become "retired," what will you do to fill your time and feel productive? Recognize we're not speaking of just a few years. If you retire at sixty-five, you may well live another quarter of a century or more. It's a long time to play shuffleboard. Recognize, too, that the elderly is the only segment of our population with no specifically defined role in our society. How do you feel about that?

Financially speaking, have you planned sufficiently to provide for a time when your income may not be as large or steady as it is today? You are probably in your most productive years of your career. More than likely you have the health, experience, skills and energy to earn the income you and your family need now and probably enough to save for the future. But saving for old age is tough. It's much more fun to buy a new car every few years. But consider the financial problems your parents may be having now and how those problems affect your life and your family. Do you want to be a financial burden to your own kids later in life? I've seen the bumper sticker that reads: "I want to grow old enough to become a problem to my kids," but I seriously doubt if most people sincerely mean it.

Your health should naturally be a consideration in your planning as well. If you have reached the age of forty, you are beginning to experience the early effects of senescence, and if you are older than that, you certainly are. You probably have some gray hairs by now. You aren't able to tolerate as much exposure to the sun. If you are a woman, you may be experiencing menopause. With senescence defined as the increase in vulnerability that the frailty of aging brings, you must acknowledge the effects of senescence on your life so as to make decisions and adjustments that will make your life happier and more comfortable as the years go by. Do you take good enough care of your body to keep it running smoothly for many more years? Are you a smoker? Do you abuse alcohol or drugs? Have you become dependent on tranquilizers? What's your cholesterol level? How's your blood pressure? Do you have regular check-ups? What kind of food do you eat, and do you get any exercise?

How are your relationships with your own children? If they are still in their teens and things are sometimes rough between you, understand that this is normal during this difficult time of transference. But if they are older and you haven't established a loving, reciprocal, adult-to-adult relationship with them, you could be headed for trouble when you reach the point where you need to make countertransference later in life. Since you are reading this book, I must assume that in one way or another, you are experiencing firsthand the problems of the Sandwich Generation, many of which result from crisis decision-making. Make plans to work with your children years ahead of your need to make any countertransference. Develop your family support system so that it goes not only from you to your parents and children, but also from your children back to you.

Retirement and feelings of productivity. Financial security. Physical well-being. Family harmony. These are four very important issues you need to deal with in planning for your own old age. There may be others you wish to incorporate in your personal strategic plan. In putting your plan together, first you must define your goal.

Every strategic plan has a specifically defined goal or goals that reflect the wanted long-term outcome. How do you envision yourself in your old age? What do you want your life to be like? If you could script your own destiny, what would it be? Try to write it in a single sentence. Perhaps it would be: "I see myself as personally and financially independent, healthy, and active when I am older." If possible, get even more specific: "I see myself traveling and living a Bohemian-type lifestyle" or, "I see myself living in a warm climate where I can play golf as often as I wish" or, "I see myself living in my present home, near my children and lifelong friends." The more specific you get, the easier it will be for you to plan the action it may take to reach your goal.

Developing your goal may take some time and lots of consideration. Buy a spiral notebook and jot down your thoughts on the subject over a few days. Play the "what if" game with yourself, just as you played it with your parents. Ask yourself, "What if I live to be one hundred? What if my financial resources aren't sufficient to last? What if I need my children's help? What if? What if?" Write down your questions and your answers. Spend time contemplating your own future. Write down how you envision yourself at age seventy, eighty, ninety and one hundred. Then synthesize all of this into a single statement of purpose, a big picture of your personal wishes for your lifestyle as an elderly individual.

To achieve your big picture goal, you need to establish shorter-term objectives that, when accomplished, will bring you closer to your ultimate goal. Let us go back to the four issues I outlined above—retirement and productivity, finances, health, and family relationships and develop some specific objectives that will lead to the goal of being personally and financially independent, healthy, and active when we are older.

Retirement and Productivity

It is common for a newly retired person to go through a deep depression after only a few short months off the job. Part of this depression stems from boredom and from the realization that all the avocations once dreamed of, such things as golfing, fishing, tennis, travel, lose their appeal once the initial enthusiasm for the activity fades. Sometimes this takes years, but often it happens in a matter of a few months. Retirees often feel they are no longer productive in society and begin to believe that the meaningful years of their lives are over. Consequently, many lose their self-esteem, become irritable, depressed, and vulnerable to circumstantial senility.

To reach the goal outlined above, you must deal with the issue of your productivity once you no longer have to get up and go to work every morning. If being a productive member of society is important to you, you will need to find some way to fulfill that goal. I feel personally that sixty-five is far too young for a healthy individual to retire from an active, productive life, but it may be the ideal time to make a change to another endeavor that is productive in ways other than "bringing home the bacon." For some, the activity is more important than the income it produces. For others, the need for supplemental income to pensions and Social Security is very real. What are the options and possibilities?

Go back to school. It is never too late to learn, and there are more opportunities than ever for higher education for older Americans. If you have always yearned for that college degree, go for it. If you have wanted to change careers but had neither the time nor the money to get retrained, retirement may give you both. One excellent educational program many older persons participate in is *Elderhostel*, which offers courses in almost everything imaginable, almost anywhere on earth. It is purely a life-enrichment program rather than a means of attaining a degree or career training. Other education you might want to pursue could be in the arts: learn to play a musical instrument or how to paint or to write short stories. Or perhaps you've always wanted to know how to sail or navigate by the stars. Maybe you'd like to learn a foreign language or finally understand the chemistry that eluded you as a teenager.

Start a second career. For those who want or need additional income, pursuing a second career makes much sense. The second time around, you will likely have greater flexibility in the type of work you might wish to seek. In the retirement years, you will no longer have as many pressures on you to meet the financial obligations of child-rearing, and can therefore enter a field that interests you even if it does not offer you a high-paying job.

To get the greatest sense of satisfaction from a second career, look at those activities and occupations that you've found most rewarding in the past. Maybe you were a factory worker or a farmer, but you've always had a real fascination with the stock market. Perhaps starting a second career as a stock broker would turn your boredom into an interesting and lucrative second career. Maybe you've always wanted to travel. A new career as a travel agent or tour guide would be just the ticket for you. A book lover could become a route driver for a publication distribution company. An electronics whiz could learn to repair computers. You are only limited by your imagination and physical abilities. If you remain realistic about the effort you will need to get a second career underway, you can open any door you choose.

I'd like to take a moment to discuss the meaning of the word "productive." Although in our society, being productive is usually equated with earning an income, nobody in his or her right mind would say that children aren't productive because they do not earn a salary, or that homemakers are nonproductive because they are not usually paid for their work. I believe that every phase of life has its own form of productivity. Children "produce" by getting an education. Adults "produce" in their careers and family life. The problem with the "P" word when we hit retirement age is that we have no preconceived notion of what being productive is for older Americans. This is the only age segment in our population for which there is no distinct, defined role to play. If I were able to assign such a role, it would be one of sharing wisdom, experience, and knowledge with younger generations. And one of the finest means of doing so is through volunteerism. In planning for your later years, perhaps you could address the issues of retirement and productivity by becoming a volunteer. There is no doubt about being productive when you are helping others in a meaningful, hands-on way.

Writing Your Objectives

Just as you wrote down your specific "big picture" goal, take your notebook out, turn to a clean page and write "Objectives: Retirement and productivity." Then beneath this, write down your thoughts and feelings about what you are going to do with yourself for all those years when you are retired. You may start with items like, "fish 'til the lake's empty," or "sleep 'til noon every day and then watch soap operas." You will probably want to do some of these kinds of leisurely activities, at least for a time—until boredom sets in. So get real with yourself. You are young at sixty-five. Young enough to want to stay vitally involved with life. Young enough to want to avoid boredom, depression, loss of self-esteem, and all the other negatives that go along with dropping out of the mainstream of life. Consider some options I mentioned above, and seriously think about incorporating the appropriate ones in your plan.

Give yourself specific objectives like:

- *I will spend six months after my retirement doing only those things I want to do.*
- *After that, I will investigate opportunities to go to (local college), (Elderhostel), (painting classes), (travel agent training). . . .*

Think about a second career. Think also about volunteering in an organization in which you have a serious interest. Perhaps you like kids and would enjoy working as a volunteer at the *Boys Club* or *Girls Inc*. If the environment concerns you, find a way to put your time to use helping an organization like *Greenpeace* or the *Sierra Club*.

You might even want to join the *Peace Corps*. The opportunities for volunteerism are wide open. You'll never have to worry about being nonproductive again.

Finances

There are many books about preparing yourself financially for your coming old age, and I don't need to repeat their content here. I can only reiterate the importance of planning ahead for your financial needs, both with your spouse and with your children. We have already discussed the pros and cons of various living arrangements, and even if your home is paid for, you will still have certain expenses you must meet.

Many people in their middle years right now have little faith that the Social Security system will survive long enough for them to receive benefits, though most have paid in a substantial sum over the course of their careers. Whether this is the case or not, I always feel it makes good sense to spread your eggs into more than one basket. Talk to your accountant or other financial planner NOW, not when you turn sixty-five. Get some sort of savings plan in place. Educate yourself about IRAs, Keoghs, annuities, the risks of your investments in the stock market. Make your money work for you, no matter how small a sum you may be able to set aside each month. I remind you again, you're probably going to be around for a long while yet. Your money will have time to create earnings for you.

Your objectives concerning finances might include items like:

. *I will meet with my accountant and stock broker within the next month to plan a new savings strategy.*
. *I will take action on their recommendations immediately.*
. *I will review my life insurance policies and update them as necessary.*
. *I will review my will and update it as necessary.*

Health

One of the first things you must do when considering your health in your later years is to understand that you will be living with the increasing effects of senescence. With senescence come two kinds of inevitable physical changes: intrinsic (inevitable biological changes) and extrinsic (controllable changes affected by your lifestyle, environment and habits). By understanding what is happening to your body and being realistic in your expectations, you can create strategies for dependable, ongoing well-being.

Intrinsic changes are determined to a large degree by heredity. Our genes are programmed when we are embryos with information that will affect us throughout our lives. In dealing with the issue of your health in your Strategic Plan, you need to understand your heredity and accept the possible effects it may have on your life. For example, if your ancestors were prone to heart disease, cancer, arthritis, or other chronic physical problems, you need to be aware of those possibilities in your own life. Many such inherited problems never happen, but if you know in advance that they might show up, you can take steps to avoid or diminish them. If you know, for instance, that heart disease runs in your family, you can take steps to reduce your risk by watching your diet, cutting cholesterol, quitting smoking, and getting enough exercise. By being aware of your heredity, you may be able to short-circuit some intrinsic changes by taking extrinsic action.

It is not so easy, however, to avoid other intrinsic changes, the dulling of the senses, the loss of muscle tone, and the general loss of some reserve capacity of your vital organs. These things are going to happen as your "machinery" begins to wear out. What you can do, though, is to treat your aging body with the respect it deserves to minimize these inevitable changes.

The extrinsic physical changes that your body undergoes also deserve critical attention, because these are things you can usually do something about. Extrinsic changes are lifestyle, environmental and habit-induced diseases and deterioration that, with a change in the way you live, can often be controlled and perhaps even eliminated. It is not always easy to change habits ingrained over a lifetime, but doing so may prevent many problems that would otherwise impair the quality of your later years. Many extrinsic disorders such as high blood pressure, some lung and heart conditions, and stress-related diseases can be controlled by eating a proper diet and maintaining a weight that is right for your age and activity level. Limiting the intake of alcoholic beverages to moderate levels, quitting smoking, and exercising regularly can also greatly reduce the deterioration caused by such extrinsic disorders.

Your objectives for building and maintaining good health might include such things as:

. *I will have a complete physical exam annually.*
. *With my doctor's consent, I will begin a diet/exercise program.*
. *I will stick to that program.*
. *I will stop smoking.*
. *I will drink alcoholic beverages in moderation.*

Family Relationships

Now comes the hard part. The first three issues are ones you can attend to on your own if you wish, or with your spouse. Unless you want to, it is not necessary to include another family member in your decisions to work on your Strategic Plan issues of productivity, finances, or health. But there is no way to avoid the involvement of others in the issue of family relationships, because getting your family involved is exactly what it's all about.

Just like you had to work to open communications with your aging parents, you will need to do the same with your adult (or nearly so) children. In many ways, it will be much easier, because you are younger, and you are not operating from a crisis. The need for countertransference is not so close and therefore not as threatening. If you already have good open communications with your children, you are miles ahead. If not, the time to try to reestablish these is now, long before you experience a crisis. Whatever might be standing between you and your children, take steps to move it aside. You must find a way to wipe the slate clean of all past resentments, mistakes and conflicts with your children if you want to write a truly successful strategic plan. Letting go of negative feelings and memories is not easy, but it must be done. It is an act of forgiveness, one of conscious release that will allow you to create a fresh, new, positive relationship with some of the most important people in your life——your children.

You may not know exactly what it is that keeps you from opening communication with your children, either on your side or theirs. Perhaps time and distance or emotionally painful events have separated you, and you have difficulty expressing your love for them. However, just as you did with your parents, you must take the first step. Let your children know you love them. Unconditionally. Let forgiveness be your watchword. Whatever they have done, try to forgive the hurt and anger it caused you. In their own reality, their actions must have seemed appropriate and, if not, they have likely been feeling badly for having hurt you. Taking the first step to reopen communications may be what they were wishing for all along but couldn't do themselves.

Forgiveness within a family has incredible healing power. When you sincerely tell your children how much you love them, you open the door to establishing a loving framework of family support that you will find invaluable when its your turn to make countertransference.

Your objectives for establishing harmonious family relationships might include:

. *I will call or write each of my children this week.*
. *I will call or write each of my children once a month.*

. *I will tell my children that I love them, every time I communicate with them.*

. *I will invite my children for a visit, a family reunion, or a family retreat.*

The above guidelines for developing a Strategic Plan for Growing Old is a simple road map for creating a plan that works for you. Take what you have learned from your own experience in caring for your elderly parent(s), add what you want for yourself and your children as you grow older, and come up with a thoughtful, farsighted plan for your old age so that your own children will never have to ask, "What should we do about Mom?"

9

In Summary

Intergenerational communication, cooperation and planning will enable families to cope effectively with the fact that the older generations are living to greatly extended ages. With people over sixty-five becoming the fastest growing segment of our population, and the over eighty-five population swelling as these elders live on and on, the problem of caring for aging parents will affect virtually every American family in the coming years.

Family life. Health care delivery. Senior living facilities. A role for the elderly. The right to die. Financial implications of longevity. These and many more issues face all of us, and there are no easy answers. We can spout philosophical postulates and aphorisms about the situation, but until it hits us at home, we are unlikely to pay the attention we should to the issue of aging.

Aging. It's not something any of us like to think will happen to us or our loved one, but aging goes on with each tick of the clock. The best defense we have against the uncertainties of old age, both for ourselves and our aging parents, is advance planning. You should never have to ask yourself, "What are we going to do about Mom?", and neither should your children have to ask that about you. You and Mom and your own children must come to grips with the realities of life—and aging and dying—and make plans together to insure a smooth and loving transition through time.

Recognizing the Realities

If you are reading this book, you have already recognized one reality—your aging parent needs help, and so do you. You have already taken an important step toward resolving the dilemma of caring for an aging parent by acknowledging the problem, as tough as it is to do so. By now, probably you will also have overcome your fear of taking action, for you have a greater understanding of what is happening to your loved one, both physically and behaviorally. You have learned that senescence is biologically inevitable, and that there is little you can do to prevent it other than to encourage your parent toward habits that promote physical and behavioral wellness. You have come to recognize that your parent's being able to handle the Activities of Daily Living (ADLs) and Instrumental Activities of Daily Living (IADLs) is critical in determining her ability to manage on her own. You have learned that behavioral changes, many times with negative manifestations, often follow the advanced stages of senescence, and how such things as substance abuse, improper use of medications or incompatible drugs can aggravate the situation even more.

You have seen that depression among the elderly is a real and present danger that can lead to a downhill spiral, ultimately resulting in circumstantial senility. You also have learned that circumstantial senility is almost always reversible through your proactive intervention.

These and more are the realities of aging with which we have dealt on the pages of this book and which now you must take in hand and act upon.

Taking the Right Action

As overwhelming as all this may seem to you, don't panic. You will be of no help to your parent, yourself, or your family if you let your own feelings of despair and helplessness get in the way. Stepping in and taking the right action to help your aging parent does not necessarily mean giving up your own life in the process. It means working together, intergenerationally in a multidisciplinary environment to meet her needs on many levels. It means opening or reopening communication. It means planning together for eventualities in advance of the need. It means understanding your Mom's generation and "where she's coming from" sociologically, as well as emotionally and psychologically. It means empowering your elderly parent to retain as much control of her life as possible, helping her to make decisions about the actions taken on her behalf, and relieving her of the fear of "losing it." That fear is often at the root of most of the problems in the first place.

You must learn new skills and perhaps change some of your old attitudes and stereotypes if you hope to be successful in helping your aging parent. The elderly today are not nearly as helpless as we might sometimes believe. They are simply people, like everyone else, whose bodies are older than ours and who, because of this, are experiencing much frustration, anxiety, fear and insecurity. If you can develop skills such as noninvasive intervention, intergenerational communication, and ways to facilitate smooth countertransference, you will be well on your way to taking the right action for your aging parent.

Planning is Everything

After you have: (1) recognized the problems that you, your family, and your aging parents are facing; (2) read and studied and learned all you can about those problems; and (3) developed skills that enable you to communicate with your elderly parent and facilitate the right action on her behalf; *then* you must plan for the future so that you do not get mired down in the situation again and again. Don't be a Band-Aid problem solver. Be a big picture problem solver. Take care of fixable things first, like overcoming circumstantial senility, rebuilding deteriorated health, resocializing your parent, and making sure her living arrangements meet her immediate needs. Then, using your newfound communications skills and noninvasive intervention techniques, work out a plan together for the future.

Plan together for gradual countertransference, on an as-needed basis only. This will give your parent a system through which she can stay active and in control of her life and affairs for as long as she can cope, and then can, gracefully and without feeling threatened, turn over to someone else those things that become too burdensome for her to manage.

As part of this countertransference plan, encourage her to prepare a living will, or even better, a durable power of attorney. You do not necessarily have to be the proxy decision-maker, but whomever she selects must understand fully the responsibilities and ramifications of the arrangement. If you and your elderly parent have established a good rapport, and if other family members support the idea, it makes sense for you to become her spokesperson should she become unable to make decisions for herself. You are her primary caregiver. I reiterate that it is imperative that your parent understand that by giving you a durable power of attorney, she is not giving up control of her life. Rather, she is retaining control and insuring that her wishes will be honored even if she is unable physically or mentally to execute them for herself.

Work together to discern what living arrangements will best meet her needs as the years go by, and if possible, avoid crisis decision-making. You will need to know her financial situation and resources in order to decide what she can and cannot afford. From this point, all the options can be considered. Involve your parent, if possible, in researching the resources that would help her age in place in her own home. Work together to identify ways to make her home safer. Help her secure any special assistive equipment that would enhance the quality of her life. Evaluate together her ability to handle her ADLs and IADLs. (Remember to keep these conversations as objective as possible, for she may feel she is able to cope better than you think she is. You need to point out to her, gently, areas in which she likely needs help.)

If you feel the best option for your elderly parent is to move into your household, don't make that decision alone. *Your* household probably is the household of others, too. Talk over your ideas with your family and see how they feel about the idea of Mom coming to live with them. Be frank about sacrifices in space, household chores, and finances that might have to be made. Have these discussions *before* mentioning any such move to your elderly parent. It would be cruel and hurtful for your mother or father to anticipate such a move only to be later uninvited!

If your family agrees that such a move would be in everyone's best interest, then invite your elderly parent, but don't insist, at least not at first. Elderly people, as a rule, like intimacy, but from a distance. The thought of sharing a bathroom with two active teenagers may not appeal one bit to your parent. Don't let your feelings be hurt if your invitation is rejected. Just let it serve as an indicator of your parent's present psychological and emotional state and work from there. Once a parent has declined to move in with her children but recognizes she can no longer live alone, she is likely to be open to other suggestions and options which you can explore together.

Alternative living arrangements, including "granny flats," shared housing, small residential care facilities, apartment-style ACLFs, and life care centers should all be considered and evaluated carefully along the guidelines in Chapter Six. Decisions arrived at should be mutually agreeable to your parent, yourself, and others in your family. This is a huge life decision, one that your parent has every right to be involved in unless she suffers from a true form of dementia. Look for the right program, not just the cheeriest apartment. An elderly person who is relocated into the wrong environment stands a high risk of becoming depressed and gradually sliding downhill into circumstantial senility. On the other hand, the right move can have just the opposite affect, stimulating the elderly person into renewed interest in life and much greater happiness.

Take Care of Yourself

You will be of no help to your parent if your emotional, physical, or psychological health is in jeopardy. In order to provide the love and support your aging parent might need, you must be able to first provide those things for yourself. Otherwise, you may not have the inner strength it will take to meet all the demands made on your time and energy. If you are reading this book it is likely you are caught in the Sandwich Generation and feel the effects sorely. That should be your first clue that you are not meeting your own needs first. Don't feel guilty when you do something to help yourself stay mentally and physically well-balanced and in control of your life. Unless your needs are met, you will be unable to meet those of others, at least not in a totally satisfying way. Take time to pay attention to your body and mind. Eat right. Exercise. Insist on respite. Stay socially involved. Participate in support groups. Learn how to say no when demands from family, friends, and even employers seem to be more than you can cope with.

When It's Over

There will come a day when your caregiving responsibilities will end. How you view that time will be a result, in part, of how you managed your caregiving responsibilities and what kind of relationship you established with your parent. If you worked together, planned together, and treated each other with mutual respect and love, the memories left behind will be cherished throughout the rest of your life. This is a goal well worth all the hard work it may take to accomplish such a relationship. Celebrate her life, let your grief cycle naturally. Honor her memory with the same communications, countertransference, and loving understanding of the issues of aging when you are the older one.

Afterword

A Tool for a New Beginning

It is my fondest hope that by sharing my experiences and my knowledge of the physical, psychosocial, and behavioral changes of the elderly I have opened a door to new understanding of what is happening to your aging parent. I also hope that I have provided you with useful suggestions, tools you can use to bridge communications gaps, engender trust, smooth the countertransference process, and enhance the quality of life for you and your patents.

Resources for Caregivers

Area Agencies on Aging

This is probably your most immediate source of information about aging-related activities in your area. Listed under the *Local Government* section of your phone directory. Although there are almost 700 such agencies nationwide, you may need to contact your *State Agency on Aging* if there is no *Area Agency* in your immediate vicinity.

National Association of Area Agencies on Aging
600 Maryland Ave. SW, West Wing, Suite 208
Washington, DC 20024
202-484-7520

State Agencies on Aging

Alabama
Commission on Aging
136 Catoma Street 2nd Fl
Montgomery, AL 36130
205-261-5743

Alaska
Older Alaskans Commission
Dept. of Administration
Pouch C-Mail Station 0209
Juneau, AL 99811-0209
907-465-3250

Arizona
Aging and Adult Admin.
Dept. of Economic Security
1400 W. Washington St.
Phoenix, AZ 85007
602-255-4446

Arkansas
Div of Aging & Adult Services
Dept of Human Services
1417 Donaghey Plaza South
7th and Main Streets

Little Rock, AR 72201
501-682-2441

California
Department of Aging
1600 K Street
Sacramento, CA 95814
916-322-5290

Colorado
Aging and Adult Service
Dept. of Social Services
1575 Sherman St., 10th Floor
Denver, CO 80203-1714
303-866-5931

Connecticut
Department on Aging
175 Main Street
Hartford, CN 06106
203-566-3238

Delaware
Division on Aging
Dept. of Health & Social Svcs
1901 N. DuPont Highway
New Castle, DE 19720
302-421-6791

District of Columbia
Office on Aging
1424 K St NW 2nd Floor
Washington, DC 20005
202-724-5626

Florida
Aging and Adult Services
Dept. Health and Rehab.
1317 Winewood Blvd.
Tallahassee, FL 32301
904-488-8922

Georgia
Office of Aging
878 Peachtree St. N.E.
Atlanta, GA 30309
404-894-5333

Hawaii
Executive Office on Aging
Office of the Governor
334 Merchant Street
Room 241
Honolulu, HI 96813
808-548-2593

Idaho
Office on Aging
Room 114 - Statehouse
Boise, ID 83720
208-334-3833

Illinois
Department on Aging
421 East Capitol Ave.
Springfield, IL 62701
217-785-2870

Indiana
Dept of Human Services
251 N. Illinois St. Box 7083
Indianapolis, IN 46207-7083
317-232-7020

Iowa
Department of Elder Affairs
Suite 236, Jewett Bldg.
914 Grand Ave.
Des Moines, IO 50319
515-281-5187

Kansas
Department on Aging
Docking Bldg. 122-S
915 SW Harrison
Topeka, KS 66612-1500
913-296-4986

Kentucky
Division of Aging Services
Cabinet for Human Resources
CHR Building, 6th Floor
275 E. Main St.
Frankfort, KY 40601
502-564-6930

Louisiana
Office of Elderly Affairs
P.O. Box 80374
Baton Rouge, LA 70898
504-925-1700

Maine
Bureau of Maine's Elderly
Dept. of Human Services
State House - Station #11
Augusta, ME 04333
207-298-2561

Maryland
Office on Aging
State Office Bldg. Rm 1004
301 W. Preston St., Room
Baltimore, MD 21201
301-225-1100

Massachusetts
Executive Office
of Elder Affairs
38 Chauncy St.
Boston, MA 02111
617-727-7750

Michigan
Office of Services to the Aging
P.O. Box 30026
Lansing, MI 48909
517-373-8230

Minnesota
Board on Aging
Metro Square Bldg Rm 204
Seventh and Robert Streets
St. Paul, MN 55101
612-296-2770

Mississippi
Council on Aging
301 W. Pearl St.
Jackson, MS 39203-3092
601-949-2070

Missouri
Division on Aging
Dept. Soc. Svcs. P.O. Box 1337
2701 W. Main St.
Jefferson City, MO 65102
314-751-3082

Montana
Department of Family Services
48 N. Last Chance Gulch
P.O. Box 8005
Helena, MT 59604
406-444-5900

Nebraska
Department on Aging
P.O. Box 95044
301 Centennial Mall South
Lincoln, NE 68509
402-471-2306

Nevada
Division for Aging Services
505 E. King St.
Kinkead Bldg, Room 101
Carson City, NV 89710
702-885-4210

New Hampshire
Div of Elderly & Adult Svc
6 Hazen Dr.
Concord, NH 03301-6501
603-271-4680

New Jersey
Division on Aging
Dept. Comm. Affairs CN807
South Broad and Front Streets
Trenton, NJ 08625-0807
609-292-4833

New Mexico
State Agency on Aging
224 E. Palace Ave., 4th Floor
La Villa Rivera Bldg.
Santa Fe, NM 87501
505-827-7640

New York
Office for the Aging
New York State Plaza
Agency Bldg #2
Albany, NY 12223
518-474-4425

North Carolina
Division of Aging
1985 Umstead Dr.,
Kirby Bldg.
Raleigh, NC 27603
919-733-3983

North Dakota
Aging Services
Dept. of Human Services
State Capitol Bldg.
Bismarck, ND 58505
701-224-2577

Ohio
Department of Aging
50 W. Broad St., 9th Floor
Columbus, OH 43266-0501
614-466-5500

Oklahoma
Aging Services Division
Dept. of Human Services
P.O. Box 25352
Oklahoma City, OK 73125
405-521-2281

Oregon
Senior Services Division
313 Public Service Bldg.
Salem, OR 97310
503-378-4728

Pennsylvania
Department of Aging
231 State St.
Harrisburg, PA 17101-1195
717-783-1550

Puerto Rico
Gericulture Commission
Dept. of Social Services
Apartado 11398
Santurce, PR 00910
809-721-4010

South Carolina
Commission on Aging
Suite B-500
400 Arbor Lake Dr.
Columbia, SC 29223
803-735-0210

South Dakota
Office Adult Services & Aging
700 N. Illinois St. Kneip Bldg.
Pierre, SD 57501
605-773-3656

Tennessee
Commission on Aging
Suite 201
706 Church St.
Nashville, TN 37219-5573
615-741-2056

Texas
Department on Aging
Box 12786 Capitol Station
1949 IH 35, South
Austin, TX 78741-3702
512-444-2727

Utah
Div of Aging & Adult Services
Dept. of Social Services
120 North - 200 West
Box 45500
Salt Lake City, UT 84145-0500
801-538-3910

Vermont
Office on Aging
103 S. Main St.
Waterbury, VT 05676
802-241-2400

Virginia
Department for the Aging
700 Centre, 10th Floor
700 East Franklin St.
Richmond, VA 23219-2327
804-225-2271

Washington
Aging & Adult Services Adm.
Dept. Soc & Hlth Services
OB-44A
Olympia, WA 98504
206-586-3768

West Virginia
Commission on Aging
Holly Grove - State Capitol
Charleston, WV 25305
304-348-3317

Wisconsin
Bureau of Aging
Div. of Community Services
One W. Wilson St., Room 480
Madison, WI 53702
608-266-2536

Wyoming
Commission on Aging
Hathaway Bldg., Room 139
Cheyenne, WY 82002-0710
307-777-7986

Associations

The *American Association of Retired Persons* (AARP) is the nation's largest and oldest organization of over-50 Americans, retired or not. A nonprofit, nonpartisan organization, the AARP has many informative materials available free or at a nominal cost. You must be 50 years old to join. If you are not yet that age, ask your parent to join. Membership is inexpensive.

American Association of Retired Persons
1909 K Street N.W.
Washington, DC 20049
202-872-4700

If your parent suffers from Alzheimer's, the Alzheimer's Association is an excellent resource for you. Many books and other educational materials are available through this organization.

Alzheimer's Association
70 E. Lake St.
Chicago, IL 60601
800-621-0379
In Illinois, 800-527-6037, or 312-853-3060.

For information specifically about Alzheimer's disease and related disorders, write:

NIA Alzheimer's Disease Education and Referral Center
#NIAC
P.O. Box 8250
Silver Spring, MD 20907

Under the auspices of the U.S. Department of Health and Human Services, the *National Institute on Aging* (NIA) has many excellent, free materials available concerning the health of older persons.

NIA Information Center
P.O. Box 8057
Gaithersburg, MD 20898-8057
301-495-3455

If your elderly parent seems bored, encourage him/her to become a volunteer. The *National VOLUNTEER Center* is a private, nonprofit corporation that works to strengthen the volunteer sector in the United States.

National VOLUNTEER Center
1111 N. Nineteenth St., Suite 500
Arlington, VA 22209
703-276-0542

The AARP also maintains a *Volunteer Talent Bank* which serves to link potential volunteers with organizations needing their services. Write to AARP (see address above) for more information.

For older Americans in good health open to an adventure in education, *ELDERHOSTEL* offers studies in hundreds of fields in colleges and universities around the world. Hostelships are available for those needing financial support to participate.

ELDERHOSTEL
80 Boylston St., Suite 400
Boston, MA 02116

The *Lighthouse National Center for Vision and Aging* can provide you with an extensive list of publishers of large-print materials, as well as suppliers of other large print devices such as telephone dials, thermostats, clocks, and talking devices such as scales and watches.

The Lighthouse
111 E. 59th St.
New York, NY 20022
800-334-5497
212-355-2200, ext. 1801

The *National Captioning Institute* and the *Alexander Graham Bell Association for the Deaf* are good resources if you need assistive devices for the hearing impaired.

National Captioning Institute
5203 Leesburg Pike
Falls Church, VA 22041

Alexander Graham Bell Association for the Deaf
3417 Volta Place, N.W.
Washington, DC 20007

Other resources you may find valuable are:

National Academy of Elder Law Attorneys
655 N. Alvernon Way, Suite 108
Tucson, AZ 85711
602-881-4005

Legal Counsel for the Elderly
1331 H St., N.W.
Washington, DC 20005
202-234-0970

Concern for Dying/Society for the Right to Die
250 West 57th St.
New York, NY 10107
212-246-6973

National Hospice Organization
1901 N. Fort Myer Dr.
Arlington, VA 22209
703-243-5900

Recommended Reading

Books

Dychtwald, Ken, and Joe Flower. *Age Wave*. Los Angeles: Jeremy P. Tarcher, 1990.

Henig, Robin M. *The Myth of Senility: The Truth About the Brain and Aging*. Glenview, IL: AARP/Scott, Foresman and Company, 1981.

Kane, Rosalie A. and Robert I. *Long Term Care: Principles, Programs, and Policies*. New York: Springer Press, 1987.

Mace, Nancy L. and Peter V. Rabins. *The 36-Hour Day: A Family Guide to Caring for Persons with Alzheimer's Disease, Related Dementing Illnesses, and Memory Loss in Later Life*. Baltimore: Johns Hopkins University Press, 1981.

American Association of Homes for the Aging in association with the National Foundation on Gerontology. *Aging in Place*. Edited by David Tilson. Glenview, IL: Scott Foresman, 1990.

Booklets

Among the many excellent publications available through the *American Association of Retired Persons*, you may find these particularly helpful:

Tomorrow's Choices. Advice on planning ahead for future legal, financial and health care decisions. Filled with solid, practical ideas and the resources you can turn to.

The Right Place at the Right Time. A guide to long-term care choices. An excellent workbook for you and your elderly parent to use when making decisions about living arrangements.

A Handbook About Care in the Home. Information on home health services which may be available to your parent and which would enable him/her to remain at home for as long as possible.

Knowing Your Rights. A guide to understanding the way Medicare pays hospitals for treating Medicare patients. Read this before your parent is in need of hospitalization.

To obtain copies of any of the above booklets contact: *American Association of Retired Persons*, 1909 K Street N.W., Washington, DC 20049. 202-434-2277.

Newsletters and Periodicals

Aging Network News, published by Omni Reports, Ltd., P.O. Box 34031, Bethesda, MD 20817. Annual subscription $35.

Parent Care, published six times a year by the University of Kansas Gerontology Center. For information write to: *Parent Care*, The University of Kansas Gerontology Center, 4089 Dole Human Development Center, Lawrence, KS 66045. 913-864-4130.

Resource Directories

HealthNet Pages of South Florida. 500 NW 165 Street Road, Suite 100, Miami, FL 33169 (305) 948-3720. In English and Spanish.